From One World to Another

Also by Rita Rogers

Reaching for the Children
by Rita Rogers and John Man

From One World to Another

Understanding the Life and Work of Britain's Most Respected Medium

....

RITA ROGERS
with Natasha Garnett

PAN BOOKS

First published 1998 by Pan Books

an imprint of Macmillan Publishers Ltd
25 Eccleston Place, London SW1W 9NF
and Basingstoke

Associated companies throughout the world

ISBN 0 330 367331 (pb)
ISBN 0 333 730496 (tpb)

3 5 7 9 8 6 4 2

A CIP catalogue record for this book is available from
the British Library.

Typeset by SetSystems Ltd, Saffron Walden, Essex
Printed and bound in Great Britain by
Mackays of Chatham plc, Chatham, Kent

Cover photographs by Lesley Howling. Other photographs, unless
otherwise marked, are from the author's collection. All photographs
are reproduced by permission of the families concerned.

To Pat, Julie, Mandy, Kerry and Mo

About the authors

Rita Rogers is a medium of Romany origin whose popularity and outreach has exploded not only since her first book was published, the bestselling *Reaching for the Children*, but as her reputation and the respect in which her work is held has grown. Mrs Rogers can be reached by writing to her at Ash House, Parkhouse Road, Lower Pilsley, Chesterfield, Derbyshire S45 8DG. Please enclose a stamped self-addressed envelope.

Natasha Garnett first met Rita when researching an article for *Vogue* debunking psychics, but felt she had to abandon her argument when confronted with Rita's extraordinarily accurate reading of her life. Natasha is a journalist who has worked for the *Sunday Telegraph* and a number of magazines.

Acknowledgements

Rita Rogers and Natasha Garnett
would like to thank all the families and friends
who contributed to this book

Contents

Preface

M Y FIRST contact with Rita Rogers occurred in June 1996. I had been writing an article about mediums for *Vogue* and had intended the piece to be a scathing attack on the psychic industry, as well as those who consult psychics. Surely no rational person could believe it was possible to receive messages from the dead, or that their future could be determined by the shuffle of a pack of tarot cards. In the course of my research I had visited over forty people claiming to have 'psychic' abilities, but I had not yet been particularly impressed. Most of the mediums I interviewed and had readings from told me little more about myself than any stranger could. Some said I would travel abroad in the forthcoming year, others said I would be happy in the future, one told me I had lost a grandmother, but she did not know how she had died, nor when, nor indeed her name. Their vague prophecies and bland generalizations did little to convert me to spiritualism.

The night before I was due to deliver the article I received a call from a colleague, who said that I should contact a medium in Derbyshire called Rita Rogers. She was supposed to be very good – so good, in fact, that she had a two-year waiting list – and actually able to give readings over the telephone. With some reluctance I made the call, dialing 141 before I did so, to prevent my call from being traced. It turned out that I was fortunate she took the call. A series of intrusive articles about her client list had made her very media-shy, as she is fiercely protective of her clients' confidentiality. 'What I do is similar to that of a doctor or a psychiatrist,' she said. 'You learn a lot about a person which should go no further, unless they want it to.'

I asked if she would give me a reading there and then. She agreed. She did say that although as a rule she didn't talk to the press, she 'had a feeling' she could trust me.

Rita told me that she discovered that she had this 'gift' when she was only four years old. She believes she inherited it along with a four-hundred-year-old crystal ball from her grandmother who was a Romany gypsy. She has spent the whole of her life trying to come to terms with her psychic abilities, and only began practising professionally around twenty years ago. On average, Rita sees about fourteen people a week in what she calls her 'reading room' for personal consultations, which can last between forty minutes to three hours. But she also gives a number of readings over the telephone because she is 'clairaudient', able to hear voices from the spirit world, as well as to see things.

When Rita read for me that evening she asked me to remain silent until it ended. That way we would avoid auto-suggestion, and I would not be able to claim afterwards that I had led her on. First of all she asked me what my star sign was – not, she explained, because she has a great belief in astrology, but because she finds them a helpful guide to people's personality types, and how they will cope with receiving the messages she is given by the spirit world. Some signs are more sensitive than others, and she would approach things in an accordingly different way.

I told her that I was a Sagittarius. She also knew my Christian name at this stage, but not my surname. She was obviously aware of my profession but she knew nothing more about me.

Rita then asked me to think of anyone I knew who had passed away in the past five years. 'Don't tell me who they are,' she said. 'I just want you to think of them so that they will come to me.' She paused for a minute before telling me that I had lost my grandfather and my grand-mother in that time, but then she named them straight away. No hesitation, no initials: she came out with their names just like that. She told me how they had died and even that I had been wearing my grandmother's ring that day, and that it had a large blue stone. She also said my other grandmother and great-grandmother wanted to talk to me, and that they had 'visited' me during the day. She said that I was the youngest of two children, and that my elder sister, whose initial was 'S', was married to a man called Tim, who had back pains. Everything Rita said was correct, but I remained silent.

She also told me that I had a young male friend who had died tragically in an accident, when he was seventeen. She said that it had happened nine years ago in March. She described, with precision, how he had been killed, and said she could see a number. It was the date that he had died. I sat bolt upright on my bed, astonished by the accuracy of what she was saying.

Without me having told her, Rita knew that I was calling her from a first-floor flat. She told me the name of my neighbour, and that there were two fives in the number on my door. She also knew that I was selling it soon and said this was a good thing, for she felt that something terrible was about to happen there. The number and the name were correct, and I had just put the flat on the market. And some months later a man was indeed murdered on my doorstep.

She said I had once had a boyfriend who was called James, and that we had met at university. She said that he had driven a red car, she knew his profession, and that this relationship had lasted two years. She then said that I had been recently seeing an artist with a 'funny foreign name', an Italian. Rita also knew that he had gone to live in France. This was supposed to be a good thing, because he was not my 'soul mate'.

Rita then told me the initials of the person who was my 'soul mate', describing him physically. She told me his profession, but said that we might never become involved. I was not to worry, though, as she felt there would be someone else. I had not met him yet but I would do so within the year, and she gave me his initials. She also told me I had a 'spirit guide'. He was a young man called Michael, and she saw him on a plane. She knew he had died in the Second World War, and that he was my grandfather's brother. 'He keeps saying "Mick", does that mean anything to you?' Rita asked. It did: that was his nick-name.

Absolutely everything Rita had told me was startlingly accurate – for as much as I knew or then understood. And as if to crown it all, before I rang off, she added one more thing. 'Natasha, there's a black shaggy dog in the spirit world, who likes to follow you around during the day. He's very loyal.' And, true to form, my beloved childhood pet had been a black Tibetan terrier, named Happy.

In a world devoid of spiritual belief, where logic and

science have done much to dismantle any romantic notions of an afterlife, it is perhaps reassuring to be told that even your family dog can make it into the spirit world. But there was more to this reading than comfort alone. What Rita told me during that hour shook everything that I had come to believe as a rational being. It defied reason and logic and yet there it was, names, dates, places, intimate details about my life that no stranger could possibly begin to know. When she told me what a grandparent was saying it was as if they were in the room with her. Their expressions, attitudes, words all came through. I did not want to believe in her, but in so many ways it was impossible not to.

Highly intrigued, it was not long before I went to meet Rita. I found a woman who was striking to look at with raven black hair and dark piercing eyes. Yet she was warm, friendly and remarkably down-to-earth. I asked a friend of hers to tell me how they would describe her. 'Rita? Words *can't* describe her. You'll never meet anyone like her in your life.'

Rita loves people and will chat away for hours, laughing and joking. But she is also compassionate and fiercely loyal.

She and her partner, Mo, share a large, warm house in the Derbyshire village of Lower Pilsley. It is set in a rambling garden filled with flowers, pets and her grandchildren's toys. She bought it eleven years ago with a bank loan. She is not in the profession to get rich: she charges around £40 for a consultation, which is modest by the standards of many I had gone to see when writing my article, and she is generous with her time.

At the front of the house is a light, airy room where Rita gives her readings. There is an armchair by the window where Rita sits, and opposite it a large sofa for her visitors. Mounted on the walls are the photographs of hundreds of children. They have all been given to Rita by their bereaved parents, for whom she has been able to make a vital link with the world of the spirit. On a cabinet is a simple crucifix, by her chair a copy of the Bible for Rita believes in God. There are no props. No pyramids. She does not use the crystal ball, although she treasures it, and is dismissive of the use of Tarot cards.

The more time I spent with Rita the more I also came to understand the part being a Romany plays in her thinking and beliefs. The Romany culture is very different to anything I know. Theirs is very much an oral tradition, one of stories, music, dancing and storytelling. 'Reading' in Romanes (the Romany language) does not mean sitting in front of a book for hours on end. Many gypsies used to grow up illiterate, anyway. Reading for a Romany means an understanding of people and their lives, what their past has been, where they are in their present, what the future will bring. Some gypsies relied on the use of tools to enable them to do this, the crystal ball, the cards, tea leaves, the palm. But for the most part 'reading' a life could be done simply by being with a person. It is as though as a people they are in tune with another sense, that they have a deeper intuition and a heightened perception. Their lore was not about science or facts and figures but to do with a spiritual relationship with the land, people, their surroundings and the spirits. They believe in an afterlife, that this world is just a journey to the next, and that there is a communication between both worlds.

Rita's grandmother predicted that Rita would come to use her gift to help people. And this she has done, by showing people that there is another world there, that their loved ones do indeed live on, that they are there to help and love us. Rita has given a great many people the hope and will to live on. But her own life has not been easy, and in many ways her gift has been a heavy burden as well. She has had to learn to use her gift in an environment that is no longer accepting of her beliefs. Some see her as a charlatan out to make money from other people's insecurities. 'But I know what I'm doing is good,' she says.

Rita's reputation and following have come about on a word of mouth basis. She does not advertise – she doesn't need to. She is booked for months in advance and receives hundreds of letters each week. From what started as a local group of clients, popping round for readings, has over the years, become extraordinarily diverse. People come to see Rita from all over Europe; she reads for people in Australia and Canada. Some people fly to England from America and South Africa just for an appointment. A Nigerian Chief even calls Lower Pilsley regularly for consultations.

And yet despite this little has changed in the way Rita conducts her work. She does not have a secretary and keeps no records. Rita's work is about helping people and showing them that there is another world. She believes that we will all reach the spirit world whoever we are and whatever we believe in, and whatever our race, culture, creed or sexuality the spirit world is there for us. While we are alive it guides us and our destinies, and is there for us with or without mediumship. Rita is not out to convert people to her way of thinking. She simply wants them to take away with them what they need.

During our first conversation Rita told me that I would write a book. To be honest, I didn't think too much about it at the time. A couple of months later it was suggested by a colleague that I should write Rita's biography. The *Vogue* article had appeared by then, and the response had been amazing. They received so many calls asking how to get in touch with her that the editor had had to hire a temp especially to deal with them. The day after my friend's suggestion, Rita called me. We hadn't spoken for some time. She asked me if I would write her book.

In 1990 Rita, together with the author John Man, published a book called *Reaching for the Children*. It described Rita's early life, some of which by necessity she recounts again here, to put her thoughts in context, but it concentrated more on her work with parents who have lost children to the spirit world. The book enabled many people who would have otherwise never heard of Rita Rogers to understand about death, grieving and the spirit. It also drew many to Rita who had lost children, and often as a result their will to live. But Rita cannot see everyone who would like to visit her. Physically she can only do so many readings a week, although in her own words, she would like to 'read the world'. So this book is written as another attempt to reach those she cannot read for personally. 'If at least I can show people that life does not stop here, that death is just a passing from one world to another, then I am happy.'

I cannot say that working with Rita has been easy. As she keeps no records of anyone she sees, finding even a telephone number can be an arduous task. There is also something quite unnerving about spending time with a woman who seems to know as much about your personal life as you do. There is no point in trying to pull the wool over her eyes. Often she will say things like, 'You were at the theatre last night with so and so', or 'You've met someone called X, haven't you? I said you would.'

Some months ago Rita and I were going to a meeting together about the book. That morning I had learned that someone close to me had died. I knew, however, that I had to attend the meeting and get through the day, and I went to pick Rita up as planned. We were sitting in a taxi when she looked at me and asked me if I was OK. I said yes, trying not to think about it. And then as she was looking out of the window she came out with a name. 'She's gone, hasn't she?' she sighed. 'I can feel her.'

Rita was right about our working together on the book. So far she has been right about most things. Over the past year most of what she predicted would happen to me has. But when you spend a lot of time with her, you tend to start taking her prophecies in your stride.

In March 1997, Rita called me one morning. 'Something has been bothering me all day. I just can't get it out of my head. I keep hearing the word 'pan'. Do you know what that's all about?' I didn't until the next day, when our agent telephoned to say that he had accepted on our behalf a publishing deal from Pan Macmillan.

Natasha Garnett

THE BEGINNING

LIKE MOST other little girls growing up in the mining town of Mansfield, Nottinghamshire, during the 1940s and 1950s, what I wanted from life was straightforward. I hoped to finish school, get married and start a family. I longed for an ordinary life. But it was not to happen that way. Simply because, I suppose, I was far from being ordinary myself.

As a child, I was always seeing and hearing things. I assumed when I was very young that everyone else saw and heard them too. At teatime I would sit at the table with my family and tell my parents what had happened to me that day, only to be scolded. 'That girl and her imaginings,' my father would sigh. My mother was less patient. 'Stop fibbing, girl! You know you're making that up,' she would say, or, 'You're romancin' again, Rita Stringfellow!' Romancing, fibbing, imagining; they were words I heard so often during those years that I came to believe them myself. But the experiences I had as a child were so vivid, so real to me, I knew I wasn't making them up. That began to scare me. Often I would lie awake at night wondering whether there was something wrong with me. I knew I wasn't a liar, so the alternative must be that I was either mad or wicked.

As I grew older it began to dawn on me that not everyone saw the things I did. I came to think it best not even to talk about them with my family. I kept my experiences to myself and withdrew into my own world. Aware that I was different, I felt isolated and alone, longing to be normal.

I was born in Mansfield in 1941, the second daughter in a family of six. We lived in a rented house in Laurel Avenue. My father, Alfred Stringfellow, had not gone down the mines when he was young, but worked on the streets doing a milk round, and cleaned windows in the afternoons. Later, he took a job at the local brewery. This was much better paid, but times were always hard for us since we didn't enjoy a miner's income. As children we never had new clothes or toys, and we couldn't even afford good fresh meat. Instead, I would be sent off to the butcher's to collect tripe and off-cuts for Father's tea. And to prevent us from wearing our shoes out too quickly (we were rarely allowed to take the bus) Father would nail thick pieces of leather on to their soles.

My mother, Madge, was a frail woman. She had been

struck by rheumatic fever when I was quite young, and she found it difficult to raise us all. She would spend long periods confined to her bed, unable even to prepare our meals or get the younger boys up for school. Because of her poor health, as one of the eldest my responsibilities lay within the home. I spent so much time washing and cooking that I rarely went to school, and it was not until I was in my teens that I taught myself to read.

Because of these difficulties at home, by the age of eight I was spending an increasing amount of time with my grandmother. Mary Alice Stringfellow lived in the town of Mansfield Woodhouse, and when I had finished my chores for the day I would rush straight over there, rather than play with the other children. Without the money for the bus fare I would walk nearly three miles to get there. But it was worth it.

To those who did not know her, Grandma Alice must have been a formidable character. She was six foot two inches tall, and must have weighed nearly twenty stone. Her hair was raven black and when she wore it loose, it swung past her hips. Her eyes were large and dark, and her compelling stare would send a shiver down your spine. Renowned locally for her violent temper, if her tongue didn't silence you, she'd be quite prepared to use her fists instead. Most people in her town were terrified of her, crossing the road when they saw her. But this wasn't just because of her rages: my grandmother was a gypsy.

Mary Alice Thompson had been born to Romany gypsy folk and spent her childhood travelling in caravans from camp to camp. When she was seventeen she was forced to leave Penrith, in Cumbria, where her family was based, to escape her father, Jonty Thompson. He was an alcoholic, and prone to violent fits of rage. She travelled south to the Midlands with her mother, walking barefoot, sleeping in barns and under hedgerows, selling flowers and fortunes along the way, and learning from her mother gypsy craft and medicine. They stopped in Nottinghamshire because her mother was ailing from the journey and could go no further. And it was there that she met my grandfather, Herbert Stringfellow. He had been out walking one day when he came across Mary Alice under a hedge bottom. She was nursing my great-grandmother, who lay there, sick, on the ground. Feeling sorry for them, and with the benefit of a miner's income, he offered to take them both in. He was quite taken with Mary Alice, and one thing led to another. What's more, he was a Romany himself, with the same dark colouring – even though at five foot two he was a foot shorter than her. It was not long before they fell in love and married.

Back in the 1940s, coming from gypsy stock was not considered something to be proud of. As a child, I was constantly teased and bullied. When I walked down the street children would cry out, 'Hey, Gyp!' My grandmother used to go out selling flowers, just as her Romany Family always had, and sometimes when I was out with her the older folk used to call me the 'Little Gypsy Girl', which I preferred. But we were generally known in Mansfield as 'Those Gyppo Stringeys', which caused my mother great offence, for although we were not travellers, and my mother took great pride in our discipline and appearance, it always implied that we were perhaps not clean, and we children were not being brought up properly.

But Grandma Alice was fiercely proud of her gypsy heritage. When she married my grandfather she was forced because of his job in the mines to become what the Romanies call a 'house-dweller'. She missed the freedom of the camp and was determined not to give up on her culture, and she carried on selling flowers and reading fortunes, transforming their terraced house on Manvers Street into a gypsy caravan of her own. There were flowers everywhere. There were bowls of roses on every table and cabinet, and from each corner hung great baskets overflowing with red and pink geraniums. Flowerpots adorned the front of the house, and there were lace curtains tied back with bows that looked like roses draped around every window and doorway. Grandfather collected clocks, and in the front room alone there must have been a dozen, all ticking and chiming away. The walls were covered in plates hand-painted by the Romanies, and on every mantle and ledge was their collection of china horse-heads. On the stove in the kitchen Grandma Alice would brew up large pots of herbal remedies, for she was a great believer in the powers of alternative medicine and healing. And when she wasn't selling flowers or reading fortunes she would sit on her front doorstep, sewing, as though she were sat on the ladder of one of the caravans she had grown up in.

At the top of the house stairs led to an attic. I called it Aladdin's Cave, for it was here that Grandmother stored all sorts of things, including her rolls of brightly coloured fabric and lace. In the centre of the attic floor stood a giant model fortress. It must have been a yard in height and at least two in length, and it was quite the most beautiful thing that I'd ever seen, with hundreds of towers and tiny windows and doors. It had been made for Grandmother by her Romany brothers to play with as a child; now she used it to store her money and valuable possessions. In the main drawbridge was a small keyhole, and with a single twist of the key every door and window would spring open at once, revealing a hundred different hiding places. Grandmother only ever let me see this happen once, when there was nothing inside. She kept the key on a chain around her neck at all times, and even Grandfather wasn't allowed to open it up.

It was here, amongst the heady scent of all Grand-mother's flowers, the smell of rabbit stewing on the stove and the ticking of all those clocks, that I felt I could be a child. Here I had no responsibilities, there was no one to look after or put to bed. Because of Grandfather's job in the mines there was always food on their table: piles of fresh white bread for tea, which we would eat with peaches. Grandma Alice would make me dresses out of her rolls of lace and brightly coloured fabrics. She encour-aged me to dance, and even paid for me to have ballroom lessons. Sometimes she would let me put on her old gypsy dresses, and I would spend hours twirling around her front room with a pair of old Romany castanets in my hands, dancing and laughing.

But my favourite hours with Grandmother were spent sitting at the foot of the chair in the front room, listening to tales of my ancestors. She told me of their travels around Europe, and about the places she herself had been to. How the Romanies loved horses. How they despised the 'Diddicoys', the Irish gypsies, believing them to be unclean. About how they liked to eat hedgehog, wrapping it in clay, so that when it came out of the fire, the clay could be peeled off, taking all the spines with it. She also explained their belief in an afterlife: that they were not afraid to die because they believed they went to another world after this one, a spirit world. And of Romany burials, how when someone died their body would be put in their caravan along with all their possessions and then be set alight. I was mesmerized by it all.

There was a bond between us that I did not have with my own mother. Perhaps this was because Mother had so many other children to worry about; maybe it was because Grandmother and I were so physically alike. Whilst Mother was small and very blonde with pale-blue eyes, I had inherited Grandmother's dark colouring and height. But I was also to discover gradually throughout my childhood, that I had inherited more from my grandmother than just her looks.

I was always aware that something singled Grandmother out from other people. For one thing, when the sun caught her hair from behind, it always looked as though she was surrounded by a halo of glistening golden light. She would often tell me she was a seer, but when I was very young I didn't really understand what she meant. What I did know was that she had the uncanny knack of being able to know exactly what I was thinking or doing at any given time, even if I was in another room. If I sneaked up to the attic and picked up something which took my fancy, or even if I so much as laid a finger on her old toy fort, she would holler up at me from down below, 'Rette!' (That's what she called me, Rette, Romany for Rita). 'Rette! Put that down at once! I know what you're doin' up there.' She always seemed to know what was going to happen next, and was never surprised by anything.

I had heard the locals call her the 'fortune teller', and I think most people in Mansfield Woodhouse were actually more afraid of what she might tell them than of her temper. For instance, she was always fiercely protective of me. One time she even went over and beat up a suitor she thought was coming on to me too strong! One particular occasion sticks in my mind. We were selling lace door-to-door on the other side of town. Grandma Alice suddenly began spouting off to a woman who lived in a neighbouring street to the one we were visiting. 'Lady, do everything that you've got to do, because you're not going to be here at this time next year. But think how lucky you are that you have been forewarned. Soon you will be with all your loved ones again.' I remember feeling a bit embarrassed by this, and the poor woman looked very taken aback. But Grandmother was right. When I returned to the house the following year, I learned that the woman had indeed passed over.

To be honest, this was the real reason why I liked to

spend so much time with Grandma Alice. I was able to tell her things that the rest of the family would have scoffed at. When I mentioned the strange things I had seen, the voices I had heard, she did not laugh or tell me off. She just sat there listening, nodding her head. For instance, I often used to see colours around people. When I asked her why, she just laughed gently and said, 'They're not colours, Rette, they're auras. You can tell a person from their aura.' If I told her I had seen someone in the street that day who had in fact died a while back, she wouldn't berate me for talking ill of the dead, as my mother would have. She would simply say, 'That's a spirit you saw today, Rette.' She didn't think I was speaking ill of the dead; Grandmother, like her Romany folk, didn't believe in death. There were no dead, just spirits. She didn't even say the word 'death' either. She preferred the expression 'passed over'. 'Because that's what happens, Rette, it's a passing from this life to another; that's all.' With her help and advice, over the years I slowly began to make sense of the strange things that were happening to me. While they still terrified me, thanks to Grandma Alice I was able to realize that I was neither mad nor wicked.

*

The first time I realized there was something different about me was when I was only four years old. My parents had taken me to hospital to have my tonsils removed, and left me there, saying that they would come to collect me in two days' time. I would have been frightened of the whole ordeal had I not made friends with another little girl in the bed next to mine. She must have been about the same age as me, and she was dressed in the prettiest nightgown I had ever seen. It was far nicer than any dress I owned. I remember it vividly to this day, white with red polka dots, and a high neck with a red ribbon tied at the front. The girl's name was Vivian.

Alone in the ward, we quickly became friends. We thought it would be funny to swap names to confuse the nurses when they did the rounds. I would be Vivian, and she Rita.

The next day we were both taken down for our operations. I wasn't scared, rather was excited about seeing my new friend again when we came back to the ward. But when I came round it was not Vivian who greeted me, but my parents. Her bed had been screened off. My parents looked somewhat bewildered and red-faced. It turned out that, around midday, a neighbour in our street had rushed to my parents' door, saying that she had received an urgent call from the hospital. At that time she was the only person in the street with a telephone. She explained that they had called because I was seriously ill; there had been a complication during the operation, and they had to get there at once.

But Vivian and I had swapped names. It wasn't Rita who was ill, but Vivian. My parents scolded me about it: 'It was a bad thing to do, Rita,' my father said. 'She needed her mother.' I asked them when I could play with her. My mother paused. 'I'm afraid you won't be able to do that, Rita. She's gone to Jesus, you see.' It was the first time anyone I knew had gone to Jesus.

I don't think I was fully aware of what death was, but I did know that it meant she wouldn't be coming back.

Later that night in the hospital, I was woken by something. I opened my eyes to see Vivian standing at the foot of my bed. I knew it was her because she was in that magical nightie. I was happy that she had come back, and I pulled back the sheets to get out of bed. But when I looked up again, she was gone. I was slightly frightened, but I wasn't surprised.

I met Vivian again a few years later, when I was eight. I had gone off to the recreation ground by our house to play, and pick grass for my pet rabbit. At one point when I looked up, I was somehow aware that I wasn't alone. I saw a child standing in front of me, dressed in a red and grey blazer, and about my age. She called me by my name, which surprised me, as I was certain I didn't know her.

And I had never seen a school blazer like that in our area. 'Who are you?' I asked. 'Vivian,' she said. 'I was in hospital with you.' 'But I thought you were dead!' I replied.

This time I wasn't frightened by what I saw. My parents had obviously made a mistake. She hadn't gone to Jesus, for she was here now, looking as real as anyone; just older and dressed in a school uniform. But when I turned my head for an instant, by the time I looked back she was gone. When I went home and told my mother about it, I got a scolding. 'Don't be silly! Vivian is dead. You're romancin' again.'

Nonetheless, after that I never really believed that people died as such and I still don't. The grown-ups had got it wrong: even if Vivian had gone to Jesus, it didn't mean she couldn't come back. I had witnessed that with my own eyes, after all.

So I learnt not to fear death from an early age. I remember being taken to see my Aunt Lizzie, who had cancer, when I was ten. She was in her early fifties, but lying there in bed, a shadow of what she had been only months before, she could have been mistaken for seventy-odd. Aunt Mabel, who had taken me, left the room to speak to the doctor, and I was left sitting at the bedside. Suddenly, a terrible noise came from Aunt Lizzie's throat. It seemed to be her last breath – what they call the death rattle. I would have been scared sitting there on my own, but at once the room seemed aglow with a beautiful golden light. Aunt Lizzie herself appeared to be sitting upright, even though her frail, motionless body still lay flat under the bedclothes, and she looked well again. She appeared to be heading towards the corner of the room. When I looked in that direction, I saw the figure of a woman whom I believe to have been my maternal grandmother. Even though I had never met her, she seemed to fit all the descriptions given to me by my own mother. It was as though she had come to collect my aunt.

At that moment, Lizzie turned to me and smiled as she passed over. She looked so happy and peaceful I could not help but smile back.

I never told my parents what I had seen that afternoon for fear they would scold me again for talking ill of the dead. Only weeks before I had got into trouble for telling them about an encounter I had had with Mr Hughes, an elderly neighbour of ours. I had been coming home from Titchfield Park, which was at the end of Nottingham Road. It was a big park, and we used to go there to play. As I crossed the bridge over the River Maun I saw Mr Hughes looking over the edge. He was a fat man who always wore a waistcoat and chain, and although I did not know him very well, he was always quite jolly when he saw me, and would make a point of saying hello. But when I greeted him that day he ignored me, and just stood there on the bridge staring at the water below, as if in deep thought. I told Mother about it when I got home. 'Oh, Rita!' she snapped. 'Of course you didn't see him. You and your stories! You'll be the death of me. You *know* they pulled him out of the Maun yesterday – out from under the bridge. They're saying he killed himself.' But I *hadn't* known. I hadn't heard a thing.

I told my grandmother about Mr Hughes when I next saw her. She sat there in her chair without the slightest look of doubt or disbelief. 'You saw a spirit, Rette,' she said, quite matter of factly. I was alarmed. 'Don't fret. They'll not harm thee,' she continued. 'He was there because he was waiting for someone to collect him.'

She then beckoned me to come to her chair and from out of her skirt pocket she pulled a yellow pouch, untied the drawstring, and tipped a crystal ball into the palm of her hand. It was three inches across. I had heard Grandmother had a crystal ball, but I'd never seen it until now. 'Hold out your hand, Rette,' she ordered. 'You know I am a seer, I can tell folk what's in their future. And you're a seer too. I'll show you. If this crystal ball turns black, it means that you have the gift too.'

I was scared but did as I was told, and she placed the

ball on my palm. At once it turned from clear to black. Startled, I jumped back, dropping the ball.

'You're a seer, Rette, I knew you were.'

'No, no!' I kept saying, near to tears. 'I don't want to be. I'm frightened, Grandma.'

'It's no use, lass, you can't fight it,' she said calmly. She explained that she always knew I had the gift, and that under gypsy lore the gift passed to the second grand-daughter.

'But what will I do?' I wept.

'How should I know?' she said.

'You can tell my fortune.'

'I'm not a fortune teller, Rette, I'm a seer. I read people.'

'Then read me,' I begged. And she did.

She told me that I would marry young, and would be a house-dweller, but that I would be widowed in my early thirties. She said that I would have four children, all girls, and that the first three would be born on the same numerical day of the month. I would live in a large house next door to a chapel. She also said that one day I would learn to use my gift, and I would help a great many people with it. And she told me that I had a spirit guide, what in those days we used to call a Red Indian, named Running Water, who would protect me and help me to use my gift.

She also said that later on in my life I would become famous because of my work.

Two

LEARNING TO LIVE WITH THE GIFT

AS GRANDMOTHER predicted, I was indeed married young. I was just sixteen. I eloped to Gretna Green with Dennis Rogers, a fitter in the mines.

My sister had had to get married and Father was furious. Determined that history should not repeat itself, Father became increasingly possessive about me. The marriage, which took place on Friday 13 December 1957, was to start with more of a release from his rule for me than a union with my new husband.

I cannot say it was love at first sight, but there was something about Dennis which made me feel secure. He seemed to want to take care of me, and was keen that we should make a life together. He was twenty-four when we met, had a job with good prospects, and even owned a car, which was unheard of in Mansfield back then. 'Who does he think he is,' Father bellowed when he heard about the Austin Atlantic, 'the Duke of Bloody Edinburgh?' Actually, Father approved of Dennis, but he

RITA ROGERS - FROM ONE WORLD TO ANOTHER

wasn't prepared to let his youngest daughter leave him just yet.

It was Dennis's idea that we should elope. It sounded romantic when we planned it: I would simply skip off from my job at the local Co-op early, with my bags packed in advance, and we would drive up to Scotland, to a place where Dennis said you could get married in a day. I had written a letter to my parents to tell them, asking them to understand. And once we had wed, we would go back to Mansfield, and back to our jobs. But the reality was of course very different.

We had to wait two weeks before we could get our marriage licence, and so had to board with two under-standing elderly sisters who agreed to take us in. We had no money, and although Dennis found some work, we were forced to sell his car. As the days wore on, I began to have my doubts. The romance of it all had begun to wane, and I felt scared and terribly lonely. I realized I wanted to go back home to my family, but knew that by now I couldn't. On the night before our wedding I lay in my own room in my single bed, staring numbly into the coal fire, longing for Grandma Alice to be there to tell me what to do. As the wind howled outside my window, the tears began to roll down my cheeks. As I reached to turn off the light, something caught my eye. Sitting at the end of my bed was a Red Indian, wearing a magnificent feathered headdress. He was in his late seventies, broad-faced, broad-nosed, with high cheekbones. He kept one eye screwed shut, as if it had been damaged. But however vivid he was to my eyes, his form seemed to be weightless, for there was no indentation on the piece of quilt where he sat.

I remembered what Grandmother had said the day she told me I was a seer. 'I've seen a Red Indian with you more than once, Rette. He is your spirit guide, he'll help you through life.' And so although the vision had initially startled me, I wasn't afraid. The Red Indian just sat there watching me.

I heard a voice in my head say, 'Go home Rita, go home.' This was the guidance I needed, but I couldn't follow it. Things had gone too far already. This troubled me, but nonetheless I felt quite peaceful and drifted off to sleep. The next day we were married, and we returned to Mansfield soon afterwards.

Marriage did not make our lives any easier, that's for sure. Dennis's family disapproved of me, and made it quite clear they had wanted better for their son. The idea that he had run off with the daughter of a brewery worker appalled them. So we planned to set up home in Glasgow, where Dennis had been offered a job, but his father contracted cancer and we were forced to move in with his parents.

The cancer made Cecil Rogers disagreeable, and I became the focus of his pain and discomfort. Eventually, the disease got the better of him, and he lost the will to live. Dennis sent me out the day his father passed away to buy a black suit. When I returned later on, Dennis had taken to his bed, exhausted by the events of the past few weeks. The curtains were drawn when I entered the bedroom, but light fell on the bed where my husband lay asleep. At the foot of the bed I could just make out the figure of a man. I dropped the suit and froze with terror. It was Cecil.

He sat there looking down on his son with an expression on his face that I had not once seen whilst he was alive. It was a look of longing and sadness, as though he recognized the inadequacies of his relationship with his son, and was now desperate to make up for that lost love. I moved towards the bed to shake my husband awake. Cecil did not acknowledge me. 'Dennis! Dennis!' I cried. My husband stirred, and at the foot of the bed the figure had gone.

'Rita, oh God!' Dennis mumbled. 'I saw my Dad! He was sitting on the bed, I swear it.' Dennis had always been very black and white about things, and did not share my beliefs in spiritualism. I didn't know what to say.

'Don't be silly. It was only a dream,' I assured him.

'But it was so real!'

'Did he look happy?'

'Oh yes.'

'Well then, what are you frightened of? I told you he would be in a happy place.'

A year later I gave birth to a daughter, Patricia. Grand-mother's prophecies were coming true. But now that I was married my visits to her in Manvers Street were less frequent. She herself had never really taken to Dennis, referring to him only as 'the man who caused all the trouble.' But as soon as Patricia was born I rushed over, eager to show off my new arrival. Grandma Alice had aged a great deal and was weak, but she had lost none of her canniness. She cradled the baby lovingly in her arms and smiled.

'When did you say she was born?'

'April 21st,' I replied.

'You can expect two other girls to arrive on the 21st, then.'

Over the following fortnight Grandmother's health deteriorated. She took to her bed, asking for me. 'I'm on my deathbed, Rette.' There was no regret, no remorse.

'Your Pat's come in my place. For when one comes in, another goes out.' I felt terrible, as though it was my fault.

'I'm sorry,' I said.

'I'm not. I'm looking forward to it,' she replied, and I believe she meant it.

'Now, Rette,' she continued, 'before I go, there is something that I want you to do for me. Come back tomorrow and I'll tell you what it is. Hurry, mind, it might be the last time you see me in this world.'

When I returned the next day, she was much worse. Grandpa told me that she was not expected to last the night. I went to her bedside and as soon as we were alone she pulled me near to her, whispering in a conspiratorial tone.

'Now, Rette, you know the fort in the attic . . . someone borrowed the key from around my neck the other night. I know someone else's hands have been on it. I want you to take the key and go upstairs. Open the fort, and tell me what you see.' I followed her instructions, lifting the key from around her neck, and climbed the stairs to the attic. I did not know what I was looking for – money, jewellery, documents, perhaps. But when I turned the lock on the drawbridge, the doors and windows sprang open to reveal a myriad of empty compartments.

I didn't know what to do. I didn't want to upset Grandma Alice on her deathbed. I thought about lying to her, but what would I say? It was no use. She, of course, knew already.

'Don't you lie to me now, Rette! Tell me what you saw. Nothing? I knew it. And I know who's took it also. And by God that person's going to pay. God don't pay his debts in coin, Rette. You watch that person suffer!'

I had never known her to be so angry. When her outburst had subsided she turned to me and took my hand.

'You're a good girl, Rette, and I want you to know something. Whether I'm dead or alive, if anyone does you any harm I'll reverse it.'

She had been my protector in life, and she would remain so on the other side. She would not stop bad things from happening to me, because that would interfere with my fate, but she had vowed to put things right again. Looking back on my life now, I can see that she kept her promise. Bad things have happened to me, and there was no avoiding them. But there has always been an antidote. 'Out of bad always comes good,' she used to tell me. 'Remember, Rette, I'll be there for you. I'll always be there.'

Grandma Alice passed over later that night. She left

everything of any material value or importance to Grandfather. Everything, that is, except for her crystal ball. That she wanted me to have.

Life felt empty without Grandma Alice, but I did have a family and a life of my own to get on with. I gave birth to two more daughters, Julie and Mandy, both of whom arrived on the twenty-first day of the month. When baby Kerry arrived some years later, our family, and Grandma's predictions, were complete.

Dennis, Pat, Julie, Mandy and I were living in a house not far from Laurel Avenue, where I had grown up. Dennis was working nights down at the pits, so I was often left alone to care for our girls. One evening after Dennis had left for work I heard a great deal of noise coming from the house next door, where old Mrs Granfield lived. I went outside to see what was going on, and met her daughter. Mrs Granfield had been taken ill with a chest cold. She lived on her own so her daughter asked me whether I would mind popping in on the old lady later that night to see if there was anything she needed. I was happy to help, and they left the door on the latch for me.

When I returned later that night there was an eerie chill about the house. I called out to Mrs Granfield, but there was no reply. I made my way to her bedroom and found her lying there quite still and peaceful. She had died. There was nothing I could do by then, except telephone the doctor and her daughter. They arrived shortly afterwards, and her body was taken to the local mortuary.

I went back to our house, feeling slightly uneasy about what had happened. I put the girls in my bed because I didn't want to be alone, and went to sleep with the light on. But in the middle of the night I was woken up. There in the doorway of my bedroom stood the old woman, with a puzzled look on her face. I stared at her in disbelief: I had been there, I had seen her proclaimed dead by the doctor, and yet now she looked full of life. 'But . . .' I started, 'you're dead!'

At once the confusion cleared from Mrs Granfield's face and she looked relieved and happy. 'Oh, thank you,' she said, as if I had just answered her own question, and with that she vanished. Unnerved and unable to sleep I got up and went to the kitchen to make myself some tea, to find to my relief that Dennis had just returned from his shift. 'Oh God,' he sighed when I told him what had happened, 'you and your bloody spooks.'

*

We were struggling financially. Dennis was forced to go back to the mines full-time to boost our income, and I got myself a job nursing the handicapped at the local hospital. Because of my husband's new job we qualified for a pit house in the mining town of Doe Lea. But although it was far more luxurious than anything I had known in the past – a three-bedroomed house with a garden, a large kitchen and separate parlour – I never had a good feeling about that house from the moment I first set eyes on it. There was no rational explanation for this, and we were in no position to turn it down. It even had a bathroom with running water: after years of splash washes in tin baths filled with water from the geyser the idea of stretching out in hot water run straight from the tap was pure heaven. We decorated the house, plastering and wallpapering it, and soon it looked like a real home – even if it still didn't feel like one to me. I kept my reservations about the house to myself though, not least because I knew that Dennis had gone to a lot of trouble to secure it for us. But deep inside I had a great sense of foreboding, as if someone was trying to warn me; as if something did not want me to be there.

There were certain areas of the house which made me feel particularly uncomfortable. In the entrance hall, by the front door next to the staircase, there was a patch of floor about three foot square which had been cemented

over. Dennis said he thought there must be a cellar
underneath it. Every time I walked over it I actually felt a
shiver run down my spine. I soon started to stride right
over the patch, which irritated Dennis. There was also a
terrible sickly-sweet smell in the bathroom, which was odd
because the suite was brand new. But it was the kind of
odour that makes you want to retch, a heady scent which
reminded me of my experiences with death. And however
much I scrubbed and bleached the room, it wouldn't go
away.

Not long after we moved in things started to go wrong.
They were small things at first: 'Nothing to get excited
about,' as Dennis would say. On our first night there I was
woken in the night by the shrill barking of our poodle, so
I made my way downstairs to see if the dog was all right. I
opened the door to the kitchen and heard a strange
rustling noise. I turned the light on and found to my
horror that the floor was covered in cockroaches, the kind
locally known as 'black clocks' because of the ticking noise
they make. The next day we covered the house with
pesticides, and scraped the dead roaches up with a shovel.
Even when the mess was gone though, I felt that this was
an omen of some kind.

On our fourth night in the house my niece, Dianne,
came to stay. She was sleeping in a room with my eldest
daughters and woke in the night feeling sick. Julie, who

was eight by then, took Di downstairs to make her some tea. Shutting the kitchen door so as not to wake the rest of the house they put the kettle on, but by the time it had boiled Di had fallen fast asleep on the settee. Julie heard footsteps on the stairs, and hoped that her sister was coming down to join her. The footsteps reached the door, the handle moved down, and then went up again. But that was it. Then silence. No sound of footsteps retreating. Puzzled, Julie opened the door, but there was no one there. She went upstairs to see who it might have been, but we were all still asleep. When she went back down to Di, the same thing happened again.

She told me about it the next day. I could tell she was upset and disturbed, so I told her not to fret. It must have been the sound of footsteps on the stairs next door, I said. And the door handle? Well, she was just romancin'. I was beginning to sound like my own mother.

The following day we went to the market in Chesterfield to buy some new crockery, which we had been saving up for. Royal Albert, white with pink flowers, was what I had my eye on. I found exactly what I wanted, and I was so pleased with it when I got it home I spent hours arranging it carefully in the glass-fronted cabinet which had once belonged to Grandma Alice. Later that evening we sat down, the whole family, to watch television together. (That set had taken a long time to save up for, too!) There was a sudden sharp, loud crack. We checked the house but found nothing. Dennis told me not to worry, and later he put the children and himself to bed, leaving me alone downstairs in the kitchen doing the ironing. I too heard footsteps by the kitchen door. I saw the door handle move down, then up. I ran to the door to open it, but there was no one there, either. Julie had been telling the truth after all. And the next morning I went downstairs only to find that three of the new cups I had bought the day before stood broken in half on their saucers, as if they had broken simultaneously. Had that been the crack we had all heard the night before? The cabinet door remained locked.

'Cheap china!' sniffed Dennis. 'That or subsidence, Reet.'

One evening a few days later, I went out to work at the hospital, leaving the girls in the care of my eldest, Pat, who was then eleven, until their father returned at nine p.m. The girls were all responsible, and I had left them on their own before. But that night I felt uneasy about it, not least because there was talk in the village of the disappearance of a schoolteacher from London called Barbara Mayo, who had vanished when she had been hitch-hiking a few miles south. There had been much talk about her in the two days since. It had been reported that she had been abducted, and that her kidnapper was on the loose near Doe Lea. So this particular night I made the girls promise to lock up behind me, and not to answer the door to anyone.

I returned home from my shift about four hours later, coming round to the back of the house as I knew that the front door would be bolted. As I reached the back entrance I was struck by the most terrible feeling. I didn't even bother to try my key in the lock: I just pushed the handle. The door, to my horror, was unlocked. So many dreadful thoughts flashed before me in those few seconds. I rushed in, past the dog in the porch, to the kitchen. Pat and Julie sat on the settee with Mandy, who was asleep. Sitting at the table were two shabbily dressed strangers. The man was tall and thin, the woman short and fat, with a pale, round face.

'What are you doing in my house?' I gasped with rage, then turning on the children, 'Didn't I tell you not to let anyone in?'

Pat said that the couple had told her they had bought a dog off me. We had been raising poodles, to sell and bring in a bit more money. 'A dog?' I blazed at the woman. 'I never sold you a dog!' I had never set eyes on this woman before in my life and believe me she was not someone you would forget in a hurry. The woman quite calmly explained that she had bought the dog off a friend, who had had a litter by one of mine. 'The pedigree hasn't been signed and we were hoping you would do it for us,' she said. She handed me the document. I stared at it trying to control my anger. It had my name on it.

I asked how she knew our address. 'We haven't been here long,' I explained.

'Oh really? How long then?' she ventured.

'Two weeks.' I replied, but I was not in the mood for small talk. Seemingly oblivious to my hostility towards her, the woman just carried on.

'It's nice. Do you mind if I look around?' And so I found myself taking them round the house, drawn into a conversation about furnishings with two strangers.

I don't know why it was, but I started telling this couple about the strange odour in the bathroom. The woman seemed interested, and asked me to describe it. I told her it smelt something like lilies. She nodded, and asked if she could look upstairs. When we reached Pat's room, which was dark as it had yet to be decorated and there were still patches of plaster and old brown paint on the walls, I suddenly saw her literally in a new light. For around the woman there was this strange golden glow, the same glow that I had seen around Grandma Alice. I felt warmth towards her. But then her eyes changed, and she shuddered. I thought she might be cold, so we went downstairs. I asked her back into the kitchen, but she turned to the man without answering, saying, 'Come on, I want to go.'

We were standing near the front door, and I felt my stomach turn. I realized that I was standing directly on top of that patch of cement. I was about to step forward when I was transfixed by something happening in the doorway where the couple stood. I thought that the house must be on fire, for a smoky mist seemed to be forming in the front room behind them. I stood there not speaking or moving as the mist came closer. As it moved forward it seemed to take form: in slow motion a vague figure appeared, with a head, shoulders, arms and legs. As it came closer, I tried to move, but couldn't. I felt cold and was unable to speak, and aware of a great feeling of fear. I thought that perhaps I might be dying, or be dead.

As the form came towards me, I could see it was that of an old lady, dressed in a high-necked nightdress, with white hair piled on top of her head. But where her face should have been was a hole of smoke.

Suddenly I felt a pair of hands seize my ankles, as if the floor had reared up and grabbed me. The grip slackened but was now moving up my legs, past my hips, easing around my neck. I felt my jaw being pulled back with a wrench. I remember thinking that the woman must have fainted because her eyes were closed, and she was slumped on the shoulder of the man.

The faceless figure grew more vivid. Solid features seemed to be forming, but not those of an elderly woman: it was a decomposing head, flesh and bone. It had a wrinkled forehead, but with no skin over the cheekbones. It had teeth but no lips, and its mouth was opening as if it were about to scream. No noise came from it though. Instead, a voice in my head screamed the chilling refrain: 'I buried my baby.'

I must have been screaming quite loudly by the time Dennis came home from work. He came in through the front door to find the children standing there sobbing, and me in this state. I remember him slapping me hard across the face to get me to stop. Everything had returned to normal. I went towards the woman, whose eyes were now open.

'Why have you come here to frighten me like this? Is it my house you are after?'

'No,' she said. 'I am a medium. I have been sent to warn you. If you don't get out of this house in two weeks, something terrible is going to happen. You should have spoken to that spirit – she was trying to talk to you. You must be a medium too.'

'I'm not a medium! I'm not!' I shouted. And with that, I told her to get out.

She returned some days later to see if I was all right, bringing with her three poodle puppies. 'You see, I wasn't lying. I really did need that pedigree.' I asked her in.

'You seemed so terrified that night,' she went on. 'Do you realize that what you saw was an earthbound spirit, one that is not at rest yet. With a seance we could see to that.' But I wasn't ready to see that spirit again; just the thought of it made me shudder.

The woman explained to me that the spirit had come to confess. When I told her what she said about her baby the woman nodded. 'You see, you're a medium. And a transfiguration medium at that. You can make spirits materialize. That's very rare – you should use it, you could help people.'

Later on, I went next door to our neighbour to apologize for the noise I had made that night, and to find out if she knew whether anything bad had ever happened in our house.

'Before you say anything, I'll describe a woman to you,' I said. 'I want you to tell me if it's anyone you know. I'm beginning to think I'm going mad.' And so I described her.

'I know who you mean,' said my neighbour when I had finished. 'She's been dead for two years.'

The woman I saw that night had been one of the first

residents in Doe Lea. Her husband had been a miner but he was called up in the First World War. During his absence, it seems she had had an affair and fallen pregnant. She had the baby, but to save herself from the stigma of her infidelity she had murdered it, hiding the body in the cellar. But her husband was killed in the war, and never came back, leaving her to become an embittered old woman. It turned out that the couple who had lived in the house before us had not stayed long. The wife, when her husband worked nights, would sit outside the house with a blanket wrapped round her as if she were too frightened to go inside. Some folk said that she had had a nervous breakdown: in the space of her few weeks there, her black hair turned to white.

The neighbours were not the only people to be sympathetic about the events of that terrible night. When Dennis told the story to his colliery managers he was at once transferred to the Rufford Colliery, and we were given a new house in Rainworth, the other side of Mansfield.

Three

STARTING TO USE THE GIFT

W E MOVED house quickly. Dennis told me to put the past behind me, but try as I might, the events of Doe Lea still continued to haunt me. It was not so much the memory of the awful apparition I had seen that night that bothered me, but the implications of it all. I realized I could no longer go on hiding from the truth; it was beginning to affect all our lives. I was different.

For many years I had tried hard to resist this reality, denying everything that Grandmother had told me. She had called it a 'gift' when she was alive, but I wasn't convinced. There was nothing gift-like about it – it was tearing into my sanity, affecting my children, driving a rift between me and my husband. Sometimes, I really did believe that I was beginning to go mad, there was so much going on inside me. I realized that the only way forward was to learn to use this so-called gift, if only to control it.

Two weeks after the move I was standing peeling

potatoes in our kitchen. My daughter Pat was with me, the dog was asleep on the floor and our cat, Blackie, was curled up in the armchair behind me. Suddenly I felt myself struck on the back. I thought the cat must have jumped on me, for I could feel claws locked into my blouse. 'Get that wretched thing off me,' I yelled at Pat. But she said, 'Mum, the cat's not on your back.' I turned round very slowly, and as I did so I felt the thing loosen. But I also saw that Blackie was still fast asleep in the armchair.

I was gripped with fear. What had made me flinch like that? It was happening to me all over again, and I froze. Pat was staring at me, terrified, and moaning, 'Oh Mum, Mum.' She called for her father, who ran into the kitchen in a state of panic.

'What is it?'

'It's Mum,' said Pat. 'She's changed . . . that's not her face.'

Dennis tried to calm her down. 'Nothing's wrong,' he said, 'she looks fine to me.'

Only years later did Pat tell me what she had seen. The features on my face had been obscured, and had changed. She said that she could see black eyes and a large pale face, framed with long black hair. She said she thought it had reminded her of the stranger who had come to our house that night at Doe Lea. But to this day I have always believed that it was most probably Grandma Alice, trying to tell me that I must at last come to terms with who I was.

As much as I loved him, Dennis was little help in all this. He had no time for it, and just didn't want to know. There was no one I could talk to except for Grandmother, and I found myself asking her for help during those first weeks. Then, one night when I was in bed trying to get some sleep, I looked up and there she was, sitting there at my feet.

'You're dead,' I heard myself say.

'I'm not dead, I'm in spirit,' she said, smiling.

'Oh Grandma, I'm so afraid of what is happening to me.'

'Don't be afraid of it, Rette. You will have to talk to those in spirit in order to help people. You *will* do it, Rette. You will talk to many in spirit and help many people.'

Then she left. Lying there in bed, I realized then that there was no point in fighting it any more. This was my destiny, my vocation, and I could not run away. Grandma Alice would make sure of that.

She was always there. Watching over me. That year, as she had predicted all those years before, I gave birth to our fourth daughter, Kerry, and I certainly felt that she was there for me then. There were complications, and it was remarkable that I pulled through. I'm sure I could see her standing in the corner of the room. On another occasion I was sitting in the garden of a pub in Skegness having a drink with my parents, when I saw her standing by the doorway. She beckoned me to come to her and I remember feeling horrified that she might have come for me. She looked sad.

'Rette, Dennis will be dead in five years.'

I didn't doubt her words. She had, after all, told me when I was just fifteen that I would be widowed in my thirties, and so far all her other predictions had come true. I felt numb and scared.

Five years later I was sitting in the very same pub enjoying a drink with my family, when she came to me again. There was no vision this time, just a voice. Clear, deep, it was unmistakably hers.

'Dennis will die soon, Rette. When the roses die, Dennis will die.'

I was filled with an overwhelming sense of emotion: I knew she was right. Dennis had not been well for some time, and my eyes filled with tears. I sat there, my head in my hands, crying.

'What on earth's wrong, Rita?' my mother asked.

'It's Dennis, he's going to die within the year.'

Dennis's condition deteriorated that summer. He had lost a great deal of weight and was drawn, but his stomach had swollen. He was admitted to hospital for tests and soon afterwards I was called to see the doctor. I shall never forget that day as long as I live – and it was Friday the 13th, not only a bad omen, but also the day Dennis and I had married.

'So, tell me, how long do you give him? Two months?' I asked, straight out.

'How did you know that?' the doctor asked back, somewhat surprised.

'I knew five years ago that he was going to die,' I replied simply. The doctor put his pen down and looked at me.

'Yes, you're right. Two months.'

Two months. It was midsummer then. My roses would be dead in September.

Like his father, Dennis had contracted cancer of the bowel. Both men were only forty-four. The memory of Cecil Roger's death still haunted us both, and knowing how Dennis hated hospitals I took him home to die. The doctors told me it would be difficult, but I wanted him to be happy. At home he had his daughters around him, and his friends took him on a final fishing trip which cheered him up, but physically he was beginning to waste away before our eyes.

On the day my husband passed away, the doctor had been called because Dennis had been in a lot of pain the night before. He came and gave him an injection, and tried to insist that Dennis should be taken to the hospital, for it was now plain that he wouldn't last long. But I refused. I wouldn't have it: I didn't want him to know how bad things were, to be frightened. I kept thinking all the time, praying, 'Please don't let this man suffer any more. Let him go.' I had to put my own feelings aside. He was in so much pain and I would not wish that on anyone.

At 7 o'clock that night, a nurse came to give him another injection. After she left I went back to his bedside, and as I entered the room it began to fill with golden light. It was so still in there, and I remember feeling overcome with a great sense of peace. I looked down at Dennis, who was still conscious and seemed to be looking over into the corner of the room. I glanced in that direction too and saw the figure of his father. Then Dennis spoke, quite clearly, although his voice was weak now.

'No, Dad, I can't go. I can't leave Rita and the kids.' But his time had come.

His head eased back on to the pillow, his eyes relaxed, and he passed away. And then from his frail weak body, lying on the bed, I saw emerge the figure of my husband. The man I had known before the cancer had destroyed him, strong and well and happy again. He looked at me as if to say he understood at last. Then he smiled and walked towards his father. Towards the afterlife.

I went calmly to the children, who were waiting in the parlour, and collapsed into the chair.

'He's gone.'

They wept and sobbed. They were still so young. They didn't have the beliefs I had, the knowledge that he was now safe and well, for Dennis and I had never talked to them about that sort of thing, and that broke me. For them Dennis had simply gone, and they would never see him again. I looked up as I held them close, and I saw him again. But he hadn't come for me, but to see his children. It made me smile, and I thought to myself: 'I'm glad you're happy, Dennis. I'm glad you're out of pain.'

And in my head I heard the words, 'Yes, Reet. Look after our kids.'

Pat asked me why I was smiling. 'It's your dad near the door,' I tried to explain. 'There's no need to cry for him. He's happy now.'

I had begun learning to use my gift whilst Dennis was still alive. Looking back now, I think that the knowledge that he was going to die played a part in it. I had to grow up a great deal during those years and face up to my responsibilities. I had started to put money aside and began to make plans for a future without him. But aside from these more practical matters, I had the urge to come to terms with who I was. I knew that once Dennis was gone I could no longer afford to be fearful of this gift, not only for the sake of the children, but more than ever for my own sanity as well. If, as Grandmother had said, I could use this gift to help others, then that was a start. I began to practise.

It started with mild curiosity really. When we first moved to Rainworth after we were rehoused, I had made friends with a woman called Margaret. She was a warm woman, someone I felt comfortable with, and she became one of the few people I could confide in. When I told her about my childhood, about Grandma Alice and her predictions, she didn't laugh, but listened intently. She seemed to believe that I might actually have a gift, and this was incredibly reassuring. Up to now the only people who had believed in me had been Grandmother and a medium, but now I had an 'outsider's' encouragement.

She suggested one day over tea that I might try and read her fortune. We were just laughing around, and I thought, why not? The only problem being, how? Instinctively, I took her hand. I wasn't sure why, for I knew nothing about palmistry, but I stared at the lines on her hand, not knowing what any of them meant, and felt the joints of her hand the way I had seen Grandmother do it. I did feel as though something was opening up to me as I did this, but I didn't know what it was, and remained silent.

I concentrated on the hand, and I thought of Grandmother. 'If I am like this,' I said to her in my head, 'then help me now.'

And then, without knowing what I was about to say, I just started speaking. 'There is a lady. Is her name Elsie?' I asked tentatively. What if there wasn't a lady? What if I was just making this up? What if this was just my imagination? Then the weirdest thing came to me. I was almost too embarrassed to say it, it seemed so bizarre. 'Does she collect eggs?'

'Go on,' said Margaret, but she remained quiet to the point where I had no idea if I was right or completely wrong.

'Well,' I began slowly, for the next thing that came to my head seemed equally absurd, 'I get the feeling she looks under hedges for eggs. And she lives near water.' Nothing I was saying made any sense to me, but it must have struck a chord with Margaret. 'That's amazing!' she exclaimed. 'That's my grandmother. She used to breed ducks and sell their eggs. She died ten years ago.'

Died ten years ago. It kept going through my head. Died ten years ago . . . I could connect with someone who was dead.

'God, Rita, you are amazing. Wait till I tell the others

all about this.' I was not sure who was more amazed by the reading, Margaret or myself.

And so news of my gift spread round the locals quickly. People were forever dropping in and asking me to read their fortunes. Over the next few months I tried to get to grips with it. I would always make sure that Dennis and the children were out of the house when I was reading – I wanted to do this on my own, I didn't trust myself yet, and I wasn't sure of the process. I certainly didn't know how I was managing to be so accurate. Was it simply intuition? Was I unconsciously guessing what was going on in these people's lives? I couldn't be. For nine times out of ten I was right, and the things that were coming into my head during these readings weren't generalizations about a person but small, obscure details and facts. I was nervous, but I obliged because I was keen to learn.

The more I read, the more my confidence grew. I was learning to understand the process, to read the signs. Sometimes it was just a colour around the subject, at other times I could feel a sensation of pain or pleasure. There were images that sprang to mind, initials that became names, random thoughts and feelings. Sometimes I would hear a voice in my head, one that was quite distinct from my own. I learnt to translate all of this, and to read these symbols and signs.

By now I felt it was time to ask my mother for my

grandmother's crystal ball. She had been taking care of it since Grandma Alice's death. But she couldn't find it. No one knew where it was: it had disappeared. So now I was on my own. No Grandma, no props, just me.

Although I was reading eight or nine people a week during this period, with what they felt were accurate and helpful results, I was hardly making a living from it yet. I didn't feel confident or good enough to charge people but now that I was on my own, raising four children, I did have to find an income from somewhere. I had Dennis's insurance money and some savings of my own, but I still had to think of things in the long term. Without Dennis, there was little point in staying in the mining town of Rainworth so I decided to sell the house. We moved back to Mansfield, and with the money from the house I was able to establish a business of my own, a small grocery shop.

The business was a strain on me, but fortunately I now had the help of Mo, and old friend whom I had known for a few years before I moved to Mansfield with the children. We had met at a dance at the brickyard. He was a fireman, and I remember taking a shine to him that evening looking at him standing there in his uniform. He always jokes now that I hypnotized him with my gift, that I put a spell on him forcing him to fancy me, but the attraction was honestly mutual! A strong but gentle man, he offered support and comfort to me and the girls. Initially we were friends, but it was not long before we fell in love.

Unlike Dennis, Mo did not object to my spiritualist beliefs. He had enough on his plate already taking all of us on without worrying about whether I was a witch or not. Soon after we met, I had explained all I could to him. His friends used to tease him when we first began seeing each other, saying, 'You'll not be able to fool around behind Rita's back, Mo, she'll know straight away.' Although I don't think he really believed in it all, he never once put me down, or accused me of making it up. 'If it pleases you, then it pleases me,' he used to say. Over the years Mo has been converted. Not by me, I might add, but by the spirits themselves.

There was one occasion that always makes me laugh when I think about it. It happened shortly after we had moved to Lower Pilsley, in Derbyshire, years later. I had asked Mo if he would fetch the ironing board for me from the cupboard under the stairs in our new house. He went to the cupboard, opened the door, and just froze. For there standing inside the cupboard he saw a man with a large bushy moustache. He was dressed from another era, in a pale suit and a straw boater. Mo went white with fright, and came rushing into the sitting-room to tell me what he had seen. It was the first time anything like that had happened to him.

'Well, what did you say to him?' I asked.

'Nothing,' said Mo. 'I just shut the door and left him to it.'

Mo never did get round to fetching the ironing board for me that day.

We sold the grocery shop in 1979. I wanted to leave Mansfield, and Mo suggested that we move to Skegness and set up a guest house. We found the ideal property in Cecil Avenue, an Edwardian terrace, near the seafront. We soon found that in our new careers as guest-house owners, we once again had our work cut out for us. I was up at six every day preparing breakfasts and changing beds. There was the cleaning to be done, and then the suppers. But I didn't mind the work: if anything it was a relief not to be reading any more, and to be treated as a normal, ordinary person. Here, no one knew about my psychic abilities – for the moment, at least.

We had only been in Skegness for a couple of months when we bumped into Norma, an old acquaintance of Mo's. We invited her over for tea the following week, and she accepted. But when she arrived that afternoon she seemed quite distraught. Her eyes were red, and it was obvious that she had been crying. She explained that her mother had died at the weekend, and although her death had been expected, Norma was suddenly overcome with grief. As always in these situations, little things trigger the emotions: she had come from the florist where she had been making arrangements for the funeral flowers.

I was standing by the stove, making coffee, whilst Norma was describing the spray she had just ordered. Then I heard a voice in my head. Without thinking about what I was saying, I repeated the message, parrot-fashion, to Norma. 'You'll be ordering another one next week,' I said absent-mindedly. It was only after I had finished the sentence that I realized what I had been saying.

I looked at Norma. She seemed very taken aback. 'What are you saying, Rita? What on earth made you say that?'

I tried my best to back-pedal out of it, but it was no good. 'I don't know why I said it,' I replied. 'For all I know they could be for a wedding.'

Deep down though, I knew that they weren't. Someone else close to Norma was about to die.

Two weeks later, Norma came to the door. 'It happened,' she said simply. 'I did just order another spray. My brother died yesterday.'

I did not know what to say. I felt embarrassed. I let her in, and we sat there at the kitchen table.

'You said it would happen, and it did,' she said, looking me straight in the eye. 'You're a medium, aren't you?'

I nodded. 'I hoped that no one would find out here, I don't want to live my life like that.'

'But I could tell, Rita. There is something funny about you. There's something about your eyes, the way you look at people.'

She asked me to read her. I told her that I hated reading, that it frightened me, and that I wasn't much good. But she wasn't having it. She told me that she had visited many fortune tellers before, but none of them had been as specific as I had been that earlier afternoon. I still felt bad about having been so tactless, so I agreed to try.

By then, I had come a long way since my first readings at Rainworth. I knew what to do. I realized that before you began a reading, you had to call upon your own spirit guides for help. Then you had to find the spirits attached to the person in front of you. I had learnt that the things I was saying during a reading weren't coming from me, but from the spirit world. I was neither a mind reader nor a prophet, but a channel between this world and the next. In this case, I was the link between Norma and her dead.

I had learnt to switch myself off from the distractions of

the outside world, and concentrate on what was happening from within. I would feel my mind start to 'open up', and at that point I would start to hear, see, and sense things. I already knew that Norma had lost her mother and brother, but when I began to read her neither came to me. Instead, I heard the voice of a man: it was Norma's father. He was telling me that he had died of a heart problem, that his name was George, and that he was with his other daughter, Norma's sister, who had died as a teenager. Everything I told Norma was accurate. None of the information I gave her I knew before. She was amazed, but more importantly consoled: there was an afterlife, and her loved ones were happy.

No trip to an English seaside town is complete without a visit to a fortune teller, and there must have been at least a dozen mediums working the Skegness seafront back then. And yet, for whatever reason, the majority of people wanting to know their destinies seemed to descend on Cecil Avenue. The guest house was starting to double up as a salon! I was fitting readings in between cooking and cleaning; from ten till two I was reading in whatever bedroom was free. I was actually beginning to enjoy it. It seemed harmless enough, and I was starting to feel that my work could really help people. It seemed that there were a lot of people who didn't have a lot to look forward to in this life, and I could offer them hope and a belief that there was something after death, a way to right old wrongs, and healing for their own spirits.

One afternoon I was visited by a woman called Leslie. She had something on her mind, and came straight to the point. 'If they were senile down here, will they still be senile up there?'

I told her that I didn't think so. Grandmother had always said that we are perfect when in spirit, and I had certainly never come across anyone in a reading who did not have their wits about them.

She said she needed to contact someone, and that it was a matter of great urgency. I began the reading and almost at once had made contact with an elderly woman called Elsie.

'That's her!' said Leslie.

'She's telling me that you have lost something,' I said.

'You're darn right I've lost something! Can you get her to tell me where it is, and please don't tell me it's under the floorboards, as I've had them all up!' she said.

Elsie was laughing and talking about jam jars, and how she liked to make chutney. Leslie was not having any of it.

'I know all that stuff,' she said impatiently.

'She only wants to have a chat,' I replied. 'You must show some respect for the spirit.'

But by now Leslie's patience was wearing even thinner. 'If we can't find it then we can't sort out the will.'

I could hear Elsie laughing in my head again. She clearly knew Leslie very well, and how greedy she was. 'Have you tried the family Bible?' I asked. 'Elsie's telling me it's there.'

'Oh, that's just the sort of thing she'd do! I nearly gave it away,' said Leslie, and with that she was off.

She telephoned me half an hour later. She had found what she was after: share certificates to the value of two hundred thousand pounds. And they were in the centre pages of the family Bible.

After a while, the readings began to dominate my life. I was seeing more and more people a day, and found that I had little time or energy to cope with the day-to-day running of the guest house. The readings themselves were physically exhausting, such was the strength of emotion often involved. And in the space of a few years their nature had changed dramatically. What had begun as a bit of harmless fun had become something more serious, more vocational. I was no longer just telling fortunes, but had learnt to use my gift to help people. I realized that the insights that I was able to give could do more than simply find lost share certificates or predict the birth of a baby. Increasingly, I was seeing people who had serious problems, people who had suffered great tragedies, parents who had lost children. As a result, I found myself spending more time on each reading. After all, how can you tell a woman who has lost her husband and her child within the same year that her time is up? I was coming at last to realize what Grandma Alice had meant when she said that I would 'talk to spirit people in order to help others.'

Soon we decided that we should give up the guest house and move again. We bought a house at Clipstone, outside Mansfield, and I began reading full time. It was eighty miles from Skegness, but both my regular clients and people who heard about me there still made the journey to see me.

We were happy in Clipstone, and I began to feel that my life was falling into place. However, I didn't really feel that the house was home. I'm not sure why, since it was perfectly nice, but I think that all my life, after all those moves, I was still searching for somewhere where I felt I *belonged*. It was Mo who found Ash House. He was reading the local paper one morning when he saw a small advertisement. 'Large old house for sale in one acre of land', and a telephone number. The owner was looking for a quick sale. Her marriage was coming to an end, she had never really liked the house anyway, and it was beginning to fall apart around her. There was also something about it that gave her the spooks. Set high on a hill in Lower Pilsley, against the backdrop of the Derbyshire moors, there was something austere about the building. She and her husband had experienced quite a number of strange supernatural events since they moved there, and there was something about the first floor bathroom in particular that gave them both the creeps.

I knew none of this when I made the telephone call to the owner. But I could certainly feel something very strong drawing me to that house. It was as though I had been intended to have it. The lady explained over the phone that the house needed a great deal of work, but I didn't pay much heed to that. There was only one question that I needed an answer to.

'Look, I know this will sound a bit strange to you,' I said, 'but can you tell me: is the house next to a chapel?'

There was a pause. 'Well, yes it is. It's adjacent to an old Methodist chapel. But how did you know?'

'You will be a house-dweller, Rette, you will live in a large house with a chapel.' That's what Grandma Alice had said. And so the last of Grandmother's premonitions had been fulfilled. A young marriage, four daughters, widowed in my thirties, using the gift to help others and now the house. We went to see it the next day: it was indeed a tip, cold, dark and uninviting, certainly haunted, and needing a lot of money spent on it. And yet I felt like I belonged there, that I had been there before, and that I must have it. We agreed on a sale there and then. I hadn't even made it upstairs to look around!

WHAT WE ARE
IN SPIRIT

I T SEEMS that death is the only truth we have in this world. Really, from the moment we are born we are dying, for every day we live brings us closer to the day we will die. Those without any religious or spiritual beliefs often feel there is nothing after this life. This makes death very difficult to come to terms with. It is especially hard when those whom we know or love in this life are taken young, or suddenly.

In this age of science and logic, fewer and fewer people seem to believe in any kind of afterlife. Scientific explanation and fact have forcibly chipped away most of our belief systems. Unless we are given proof that something exists we remain sceptical or suspicious of it, and for most of us, death is therefore the full stop that ends our lives. There is nothing afterwards; there is only one life.

But I believe that there is much about this life, and death, that we cannot explain – perhaps because we are not supposed to. Death is inevitable, but because our understanding of it is limited, we tend to fear it.

Actually, 'death' is not a word I like to use. The experiences I had as a child convinced me right from the start that after death we live on – albeit in another form. For me, death is simply a passing, a passage from this world to another. Life does not stop with the grave, it comes on. Death does not signify the end, it is the beginning of a different phase of life, a spirit life. The day on which we die does not mark the final day of our life but the start of another – it is our second birthday.

It was not just the strange visions and experiences I had as a child that convinced me of this. Nor was it simply the teachings of my grandmother. My views on death and an afterlife were shaped by my own, first-hand experience of dying. This is a phenomenon that is sometimes described as a near-death, or out-of-body experience.

When we were still living in Mansfield, I suffered a mild stroke. Mo had taken me to a dance and I remember feeling very drained and weak by the time we got home. The months leading up to that night had been extremely stressful for us both and the particular strain of running the grocery shop and looking after the family too had left me feeling quite low and tired. As soon as we got home after the dance, I went to the kitchen to put the kettle on. I took my coat off and was about to hang it over a chair when I was gripped by an acute pain in my chest. It seemed as if my heart was being squeezed tightly, to the point where it felt as though it was on fire. I didn't cry for help, because I couldn't. I couldn't move at all! I stood there, doubled up, gasping. Then I lost control and fell to the floor. By the time Mo came in and realized what was going on, I was unconscious. He rushed to my side and began trying to revive me – as a fireman, he was equipped with first-aid skills.

Even though I was unconscious, I do not recall *any* lost moments. I remember clearly that as soon as I fell I still felt as though I was somehow able to sit up, and felt absolutely fine again. The pain had completely disappeared. Feeling OK, I felt I had stood up and walked towards the door. But as I got there I turned, for I wasn't really sure where I was going, and looked for Mo. I was surprised to see him kneeling on the floor, crying beside the body of a woman. He seemed to be pummelling her chest. I had no idea who she was, and was confused. What was he doing? I called out to him to ask what was going on, but soon I realized he couldn't hear me. Through his sobs I heard him say, 'Oh God, Rita, please don't die.'

And then it came to me. It was *me*. I was looking at myself. The only conclusion I could draw from what I was seeing was that I must have passed over. Mo was checking for my pulse, listening for breath, trying not to panic. I could hardly begin to come to terms with what I felt I was witnessing. That body *couldn't* be mine, for I was there, on the other side of the room. Looking down, I could see myself, and I felt fine – better than I had for years: no stress, no worry, full of energy.

At that moment I felt myself being snatched from where I was standing in the kitchen into a dark tunnel. It was almost black and I was being pulled very quickly so I couldn't really see where I was. At the end of this tunnel was a pin-point of very bright light, which I seemed to be heading towards. I wasn't scared or worried, my only conscious thought was the light. As I approached it, I could hear my name being called, over and over again: 'Rita, Rita.' It was not one voice, but a chorus of people, all calling my name. Then I reached the end of this tunnel and was pulled into the light, and I was suddenly overwhelmed by a feeling of immense happiness and joy.

Although I couldn't feel anything under my feet, nothing concrete, I was standing. It was as though I was dreaming, and yet what lay before me seemed so vivid and real. I seemed to have been transported to the most beautiful landscape I had ever seen, with rolling hills, green hedgerows and trees. It was like a summer's day, for the light was so bright there, almost luminous. There were people before me, strolling; children were playing. But a hedge separated me from this scene. Set in the middle of it was a plain wooden gate, where Grandma Alice, Dennis and my aunts, Lizzie and Ivy, stood, leaning on the top bar. They had come to meet me. I didn't feel frightened or sad, just happy. I hoped they would open the gate and let me in.

But they didn't. Then Dennis spoke, 'Rita, you're not dead.' And at that moment, before I had even a chance to respond, I felt myself being sucked backwards, away from the light, through that dark tunnel again. As I came out of the darkness of the tunnel I fell gently to my feet, and then there I was in my kitchen again, by the door. Without giving it a second thought I walked towards my body lying there next to Mo, and re-entered it with apparent ease. Then I blacked out.

The next thing I was aware of was coming round and seeing Mo above me, still pounding my chest. It felt sore, but the acute pain had gone. Seeing me come round, Mo told me to lie still while he telephoned the hospital. I lay there on the floor, feeling fine. My body had survived but I knew that my spirit had been changed for ever. Whatever pain death might involve, I knew now that it was counter-balanced by the joy and happiness of what lay thereafter.

*

Our fear of passing away originates not only from a terror of the unknown but also from the inability to imagine a life apart from this one. Spiritual and religious beliefs might provide a rhetoric and a structure of symbolism to support the idea that there is also another system at work, but describing what it is to be in spirit, and what a spirit life entails, is hard. It goes against everything that we have been taught.

Our lives are so deeply rooted in the material that it is quite difficult for the lay person to imagine that it is possible to exist away from this world: 'that we can carry on living without the shell of our physical body, that the self goes beyond the mortal form, that we can inhabit a world that it is not tangible or concrete. That it is possible to communicate with spirits seems improbable, because it defies anything that we have come to know in this life.

When we die our physical body is discarded because it has become obsolete, and is no longer of any use to us. We enter a spiritual state, but we do not *become* spirit as such, because we already have spirit *within* us. Passing over is a continuation of life, for at the moment of our conception spirit, or soul, enters our physical form. So in death as we understand it, it is only part of us that dies, the physical part. Our spirit, or soul, is still very much alive; we are still the same person we were in this life, we have the same characteristics. But we have become another form. It is a bit like the metamorphosis of the caterpillar to the butterfly. Death, therefore, is just a chrysalis. When you pass over you will still be the same individual you were when you were alive, the only difference being that you will have abandoned your physical body.

In death, then, the only sadness should be for those who are left behind. When we grieve it is for ourselves, for the life we must confront without the person who has passed over. We should not mourn their passing because they are still very much alive, only in a better world, one where life is richer and fuller. This is why I always say, 'The grave is for you and not for them.' Funerals, graves, crematoriums, all these are for the living. They stand as symbols for the life we lived here on earth. But we should not look there for the one who has passed away. They are not there. They are everywhere, all around us.

In spirit we seem to replicate the body we had in this life. The spirit body is an image of our own body, only it does not reproduce disease, infirmity, handicap (whether physical or mental) and it does not age. As Grandmother used to say, 'We are all perfect in spirit.' No matter how much we have suffered at the time of our death through illness, accident or old age, we shall be restored to our true selves when we pass over. I witnessed this with my own eyes when I saw the spirits of my husband, Dennis, and my father-in-law, Cecil, leave their bodies after they had passed over. Although both men had died of cancer, the illness leaving them both shadows of their former selves, in spirit they seemed strong and healthy, appearing as they had been in the prime of their lives.

Those who have physically suffered a great deal in this life should not fear passing away. I believe they should look forward to it! For instance, a person who has been heavily disabled in this life will be freed from the shackle of their physical body in the next. Similarly, a person who is mentally handicapped will be able to communicate freely in the afterlife, things are so different there. I read for a mother who lost her daughter when the child was only seventeen years old. The girl told me, in a clear, articulate voice, that when she had been alive she had 'not been perfect'. She wanted her mother to know that she was happy and not to worry. She told me that when she was alive she had suffered from Down's Syndrome. Through the gift of transfiguration, I was able to make her actually appear for her mother. At the end of it I realized that the woman was obviously very moved. I asked her if she was all right. 'Oh yes,' she said, 'I am, now that I have seen her.' She explained that when she had seen the image of her daughter across my face she recognized her instantly.

But she told me that her daughter bore none of the physical side effects of the disease. 'She looked even more beautiful than ever before,' she said.

One question I am often asked during readings is what we will look like when we reach the spirit world. I recently read for an elderly woman who must have been in her late nineties. She had lost her husband in the First World War and had never remarried, such was her love for him. When she came to see me though, it was not to contact him, but to ask me what she would look like when *she* passed away and reached the spirit world. She had waited all her life to be reunited with him, and was concerned that when she reached the spirit world and saw him, she would look old and wrinkled, whilst he would look like a young man. She was worried he might not love her any more.

She need not have worried. The spirit body, unlike the human body, is not a fixed form. We view it subjectively. When we look on that person we see an image of them which is how we knew them in the prime of our relationship with them. For example, a mother who dies will look to her children as they remember their mother, to her husband as his wife, to her grandchildren as their grandmother. We are probably shown that person in the way that we will best understand how happy and peaceful they are, and the way it will mean the most to us. Furthermore, nwhen we reach the spirit world, all our worries leave us, so we should not be concerned about how we, or anyone else, looks. And the love we have for each other there is unconditional.

Just because we cannot see, hear or feel the presence of spirits does not mean that they are not with us. The average person, without clairaudient skills (such as mine, when I hear the spirits talking to me) or a clairvoyant ability (where the medium actually sees the spirit, and is often futurized), cannot hear or see them because, spiritually, they are deaf and blind. Yet even if we cannot sense them, it is important to realize that spirits are always with us. They visit us throughout the day and the night.

You do not need to consult a medium to be with a spirit, although that is a means of communicating with them. At birth, we are each appointed with our own spirit guide. Spirit guides are usually connected somehow to the person they watch over, whether a parent, a relative or a friend. But even if you have not known anyone who has passed over within your own lifetime, you do still have your own guide. They may be a distant relative or even an ancestor, and they act as your own personal, invisible detective, on call twenty-four hours a day, acting as guardian angels.

But for most of us the loss of a close friend or relative can leave us feeling quite alone. Grief can make people's lives feel empty, futile and meaningless. Robbed of the physical presence of a loved one, the person left to grieve may feel as if they want to stop living now they no longer have that person in their life. People who have lost someone very dear to them often ask the question, 'Why did you leave me?' It is normal during the grieving process for a person to feel abandoned, and part of my work as a medium is to assure people that this is not the case. The person who has passed over is still very much with them, on a daily basis.

During a reading, a spirit, communicating through the medium, will try to get this across. They do this in two ways. First, they assure the person who has visited the medium that they are indeed someone known to them who has passed over. They do this by giving the medium facts about themselves, and also the person who wishes to make contact with them. Second, they offer them information which proves that they still visit them, even though they have gone. At this stage they will talk of changes or events that have happened since they passed over. Spirits are only too aware of our scepticism down here, which is why I believe that they offer us such seemingly banal information about our day-to-day lives. A spirit who is distantly related to us will give information about our family. The most usual way for them to do this is to name people close to us, whether they are alive or have passed over. During the reading, I find they will throw initials or whole names at me. They do this to reassure us that we are speaking to someone we know. They might begin by telling us what colour car we drive, what work we do, or be even more specific. And to let us know that they are still with us, they may comment on what we have been doing since they died. A child in spirit is likely to notice changes made around the house, or that we have a new pet; a husband might comment on how his wife has changed her hair, or that she has been having problems with the builders. They often tell me when the family last visited the grave or crematorium.

This may all seem very trivial to someone who has not visited a medium before, but for those who have lost a loved one there is an incredible amount of value in the smallest message or anecdote. These small but specific details are what make the difference, and these facts can convince the most determined disbelievers that they are indeed in the presence of the person they have lost. I once read for a woman who had travelled from Israel to see me. She arrived for the reading with her husband in tow. He was a Rabbi, and was wearing a black skullcap. He looked quite uncomfortable in my reading room, and seemed to be uneasy about the session. I don't think he believed in it, but his wife, who was very upset about something, had insisted that he come with her for support. Almost immediately, I picked up a young man in spirit who had died very tragically. He was their son, and he had been killed in a motorcycle accident. I told them that he had only had the bike for a couple of days. He said that he was only seventeen. He explained that he had been due to go into the military service. He also told me what he had been studying before he died, that he wanted to be a teacher because he loved children. He knew his mother had absolutely adored him. I had got halfway through the reading when I came out with the son's name. 'Is it Moshe?' I had to ask them, for I had never heard a name like that. The Rabbi did not answer but nodded. Then he said, 'Having listened to what you have said, I am going to have to re-evaluate the way I look at my beliefs, because I know that is my son you are talking to, Mrs Rogers.'

It is not just the people who are left here who go to mediums to make contact with their loved ones. Often spirits will go to great lengths to communicate with the ones they have left behind. They do this because they are aware of the great grief and unhappiness that their passing has caused, and they will try and bring that person to a medium in order to let them know they are safe and well, to tell them not to worry any more. There are two cases from my experience which strike me as interesting. Both involve the spirit of a child who has passed over.

Ryan was only seventeen when he was killed in a road accident. Lara was just four and half when she passed away. She had suffered from a heart condition. Her mother, Beverly, had not tried to contact me when her daughter passed over, but somehow Lara brought her to me. Ryan was equally determined, leading his mother, Pat, who lived in Johannesburg, South Africa, all the way to me. Like Beverly, Pat had been devastated by the passing of her child, and was learning to cope with his death in her own way. But she never had any intention of deliberately setting out to consult a medium – let alone one who lived on the other side of the world.

I will tell both their stories in their mothers' own words.

RYAN

Ryan was only seventeen when he was killed in a road accident. His father and I, and indeed all his family and friends, were devastated by this loss. He had always been a wonderful son. He was good looking, bright, and had beautiful manners. He was popular amongst his own contemporaries and had a large group of friends. Of course, it is natural for any parent to think that their own child is special, but you couldn't help but like Ryan on first meeting him. He had a lot of charm.

Looking back, it is as if Ryan wanted to reach us. He really was drawing us in. I had never been a great reader at all, and since Ryan's death I could barely even think about working, let alone putting my mind to a book. But one afternoon when I was out shopping with a friend in Rocky Street, Johannesburg, I walked into a second-hand book shop. I had no intention of buying anything and I was just standing there, staring into space, when one particular book caught my eye, and I found myself pulling it down toward me. It was by a woman who I had never heard of, Rita Rogers. I read the back of the book. It said that she was a medium, and that she had helped parents who had lost children. I bought it.

I read the book from cover to cover in just a few days. After I had put it down, I was filled with this desire to meet Rita. I just have to contact this woman, I thought. My husband and I had never been to a medium before. We thought we weren't 'those kind of people', and in South Africa it's not the sort of thing people talk about. I didn't know her address, but I wrote to her anyway. How it got there I'll never know. I think that on the envelope I just put her name, and the county where she lived.

My husband Colin thought I had lost my marbles. He was

very much against the whole thing. We had been coping with Ryan's death in the conventional way, and he thought this might cause a setback. But then we heard from Rita! She gave us an appointment for a telephone reading; I was nervous, but desperate to go through with it. Colin reluctantly conceded.

The first thing that Rita told us was that we had lost a son. We gave her no prompting. She said he had died in a tragic accident; that he was young. She said she had an initial but she couldn't be quite sure, because she didn't understand his accent. I think Colin was sceptical at this point. Maybe he thought Rita was just hazarding a guess. And then she said, 'Is it B or R, because I think I'm hearing Ryan, but it could be Brian?' Well, that was that. There was my son talking to Rita! I knew it was him, that he was there. To hear what he was saying, the details he gave us about his flat, the family, naming his friends, his girlfriend, there was no mistaking him. Even the way Rita was using words was the same as he had used them.

We were so sure that it was Ryan we were talking to, we booked an apointment to come and see Rita in person. It took us two years to save for the trip over to England, but we knew we had to go. I believe that Ryan meant us to meet Rita. I really feel that he led me to that shop that day, urged me to pull her book off the shelf. It was as if, watching what we as a family were going through, he had to let us know that he was OK.

LARA

There is no one except Lara who found Rita for us. I had never heard of Rita Rogers, but two weeks after Lara had passed away two acquaintances of my mother's went to see Rita. Rita was reading for them when she said that she was getting a little girl in spirit, and asked them if they knew her, but they said no. However, the little girl wouldn't go away, so Rita asked what she wanted, and she told her that she wanted to talk to her mummy. Rita told them that she was very fair-haired, and that although the child was very young, she 'talked old'. Now, the one thing people used to notice about Lara was how she liked to chat away. Although she was very young, she could sometimes sound like an adult. 'Talking old' is exactly how we used to describe it. And she was very particular about things; with Lara everything had to be just so.

As it was now clear that this little girl was not going to go away, Rita carried on talking to her. She got the initial L of her name. Rita also said that when the little girl had passed away it was not because of an accident, but because she had a problem with her heart – she had suffered from a heart spasm. Then she said that she knew these people were going to see her grandmother later that day. At that point my friends realized that it must be Lara, for they were going on to see my mother, and they knew that her granddaughter had recently passed away.

Rita told them that she knew many tears had been shed over this child and that the spirit was telling her that she thought Rita could help us.

Later that day my mother telephoned me and told me what had happened. I was uneasy about this sort of thing, but the friends had made a tape of their reading, so I was able to listen to it first before I made up my mind about what to do.

Lara was only four and half when she passed over. We had been coming back from church. I was standing on the doorstep, behind Lara, trying to get the children in to the house, when she fell. I managed to catch her in my arms. Her eyes were shut, and it seemed as though she was having some kind of fit. I shouted for help, my mother called for an ambulance and the local doctor, but Lara had already stopped breathing. The doctor tried to massage her heart, but it was no use. I called my husband, Jan. We drove to the hospital but when we got there it was too late. The hospital didn't have an explanation; they carried on doing tests for some time afterwards but found little, which it was very difficult to deal with. We needed reasons. When someone passes away you are always asking yourself why, and if there is anything you could have done to prevent it from happening.

People often ask how we coped. I'm not sure. The fact is that you have to – you have no choice. We also had two other children to care for. Daryl was two and Kiri was only four months old then and if it wasn't for them I think part of me would have wanted to follow Lara. How do you explain these things to children that age, when you can't make sense of them yourself?

A week after she passed away I was on the telephone to a friend when I experienced a warm feeling round my back and shoulders as if I was being hugged very gently. I felt it was her. I had always believed that when someone passes over they are always still with you. But I had never been to a medium.

The taped reading convinced me that Rita was really communicating with my daughter. And so we went to see her. We were both extremely nervous but once the reading started I felt so much better. It was as though all my fears about how Lara was were lifted. Rita said that she had found an elderly lady with a young girl. She said that she felt it was one of our mothers, and that this lady was looking after Lara, although at this stage she hadn't given us her name. She then said Jan hadn't brushed his hair that morning — and it was always a standing joke in our house that Jan never brushed his hair. She started talking about when she passed away, and where we had all been. She described the vicarage, saying that we had been to church first. She also said that she had had a heart spasm. By the time we had gone to see Rita, it had been confirmed that Lara had suffered from a palpitation of the heart.

We have seen Rita regularly since then. But there was

something about that very first reading. I felt uplifted afterwards to know that Lara was happy, being cared for, and still with us. And I believe this is what Lara wanted us to feel, and why she brought us to Rita.

Five

THE SPIRIT WORLD

ONE REASON why we have such difficulty with the concept of passing away is that we have little, or even no, idea or evidence of what lies on the other side. Different cultures and religions offer their own descriptions of what the afterlife is like. Some suggest that there is a heaven for the good, a hell for the bad. Other religions embrace the idea of reincarnation into this world. Whatever we choose to believe in, and however strong that conviction is, it is natural still to fear passing away, for it is removal away from everything that we know. However bad this world is, given the choice most people would prefer to stay here than move on into the unknown. And even if we do believe that the spirit exists beyond death, then it is hard to imagine in what capacity, for we are so used to thinking of experience in physical terms. I am often asked, particularly in the case of those who have lost children, whether the person who has passed over is cold. This is understandable, since the process of death does affect the temperature of our bodies. But what we have to begin to realize is that over there we are no longer within that body, that we have moved on, and that we are not necessarily susceptible to the same physical sensations we knew in this world. Most of the images that we associate with passing away are related to the body that is left behind and to the grave: coldness, darkness, isolation and decay. But if we begin to try to imagine what it was like beyond our own physical being, the idea of dying might be easier to live with.

It is difficult describing the afterlife in three-dimensional terms. It is not *like* this world, it is not concrete or solid. It has no boundaries as such, no geographical position. It is certainly not made out of white clouds or fire and brimstone, and it is neither above nor below us. It just *is*. The afterlife is in many ways a state of mind and by that I do not mean that it does not exist or is just a figment of an active imagination, but that it is more akin to a higher level of consciousness than a place we may have visited in this world. It is comparable to what happens when we go to sleep and dream. Then we move away from our physical bodies, into another plane of consciousness, and are able to travel into another world. We still seem to look the same, we recognize people, and we are capable of emotion, yet during these dreams nothing that we experience affects our body physically.

We are able to do all these things, have all manner of experiences, go to places and yet do it all without our bodies. Life in spirit is like another such level of consciousness.

The world I am describing is pieced together from the communications I have had with spirits. I do not claim to have the whole picture – it is only a glimpse. All I have are the fragments of experiences and visions that have been passed on to me. We cannot measure spirit life in the way that we measure this world; it is difficult to describe, or even imagine, a world that is superphysical and superior to what we know here, a life that does not know our normal limitations and dimensions.

When we die it is not as though we are transported to another universe. The spirit world does not seem to have any fixed location or boundaries. Spirits seem to be free to travel between both worlds, and the messages I receive indicate that they spend time in their own world but that they are capable of visiting us here. During a reading, for example, a spirit might allude to something that has happened since their passing from this side. It could be that they have noticed a change around the house, that something has been removed from their bedroom, that their family has bought a new dog. These are small pieces of information, but ones that add weight to the notion that spirits are always with us, although they have their own lives there, too. The spirit who communicates with us during a reading may not be one constantly watching us, but they transmit messages on behalf of the whole spirit world, coming to us in a form we will understand.

The spirit world may not be a geographical place, but it does appear to have a structure. My understanding is that there are seven different astral planes in the afterlife, each reflecting the level of our spiritual being. Most psychics seem to agree with this, and I believe I have been shown them. The first plane is the lowest, and is reserved for those who have, without any degree of remorse, committed heinous crimes in this life; the second is for those who have done wrong but have shown signs of regret. And so the structure continues. The seventh plane is for those who have reached a level of spiritual perfection. So there are no heaven and hell as such; as Grandma Alice used to say, 'This here is your hell, you'll not get worse than this. And you make your own heaven.' The structure reflects the way we have lived our lives here, and when we die we gravitate to the spiritual sphere for which we are suited. Our lives here are our spiritual passports.

The spiritual hierarchy is not fixed. When we enter the spirit world on a particular plane, the idea is that we grow and improve spiritually until we eventually reach the seventh plane. From what I have gathered, most adults enter on the fourth plane. A child whose life has been cut short, a person who has suffered a great deal either physically or mentally in this world, may go straight to the sixth or seventh plane. The idea is that we keep moving upwards.

In spirit we are constantly evolving, and what we are spiritually is shaped by our emotions, our words and our actions here, and there. But once we are in that world, we do not move down the structure. We move up as we learn more of what it is to be in spirit, part of which is doing good deeds through communicating with those in need still in this world. But there is nothing that we can do in spirit, no crime to commit, no wrong to be done to another, that would send us down to another plane.

Should we commit murder or rape or some other terrible crime we will pay for that up there by starting out on the lowest rung of the spiritual ladder. Although we have the benefit of being in spirit, we do not enjoy the higher planes, and are unable to travel back to this world, either, until we learn more. This is why spirits do not tend to be vengeful, because they are secure in the knowledge that whatever an individual has done in this life, even if they have escaped punishment, they will be judged when they pass over. If you had been punished down here for a crime that you did not commit then you will go to a higher level on that side. We make our own heaven and our own hell. If you have been a good person in this life then you have nothing to fear, for you will not get lower than the pain and suffering you have now.

But even though there is a structure of this sort, there is no geographical separation between the planes. Spirits are free to travel here and there; each plane blends into the next. And even if your loved ones inhabit another spiritual plane, you will still be with them.

Grandma Alice used to say, 'Don't imagine a man in a big white robe waiting for you when you die, Rita, he won't be. I'll be there waiting.' When we pass over, it seems that we are met in the spirit world by the people who have known and loved us in this life but who have gone before us. Should you die not knowing anyone who has passed over then you will be met by an ancestor or someone spiritually connected to you. It seems that those in spirit know when our time has come and prepare for that. We do seem to be immediately reunited with those we have known who have passed over before us, and there are no problems with recognition or finding people. They are there for us, to be with us, as though they have been waiting for that moment to come.

There are no sexual relations in spirit since we do not reproduce in that world, but there is immense love. Lovers are reunited, and we all find what I call our soul mate, even if we do not find them in this life. Those who have been childless here will be given spirit children and babies to care for until they are reunited with their parents.

Life in spirit is full of activity, and there are opportunities for all. We do have occupations, but because there are no economic factors governing that world, we do not work for material gain. As a result we tend to gravitate towards things which are more creative, perhaps better suited to us than the jobs we had in this life. We tend to do things in which we can express our natural gifts and talents.

There are no nationality divisions in spirit, since nationality does not exist there, so there are no language problems. Spirits always speak to me in a language I can understand, although sometimes in an accent to give me a clue as to who they are, or to help them be identified for the person for whom I am reading. Language in spirit embraces a totality of thought and ideas which is superior to what we have known in this life. Deception, lying, cheating are all impossible, and there are no secrets.

From the messages I have received, spirit people seem to live in houses with the ones they love. These are not material houses as such, as far as I can tell; they are not tangible as bricks and mortar are to us on earth. Similarly, from the apparitions I have seen, spirits seem to wear clothes. But in both cases perhaps this is more a subjective projection of how we expect spirits to live and what they look like than evidence of spiritual domesticity or haute couture.

Spirits' ideas of time seem to be very different from our own. They sometimes give specific dates of things that have happened in the past during a reading, but when it comes to the present or the future they appear vague. For example, they might say that your wedding, or a birthday, was on 5 March 1970, but they do not tend to say 'twenty-seven years ago.' What seems to be a long time in our world goes quickly in theirs. They do not feel that they are having to wait a long time for a loved one to pass over and join them, and although they all seem to move towards their optimum age, they do not experience the same sense of passage of time as we do.

There is no ageing in the physical sense, but a growth toward spiritual maturity. I have noticed through my readings that children who die do go on to grow up in spirit. From what I have learnt, they grow until they reach the age of twenty-one, the accepted view of maturity. During this time they will be cared for by other people, unless their parents are also in spirit, and they seem to receive some kind of education. Often during readings they will tell their family of what they have been doing or learning in spirit. And just as the young mature, so the old grow younger in spirit; in spirit, we all exist in our prime.

Sally Anne was fourteen when she suffered fatally from a brain tumour. Her mother, Angie, felt quite lost when she passed away, and started coming to me for readings. I think her story is a good illustration of what life in spirit is all about.

As soon as I began the reading for Angie I realized that she had lost someone very close to her. You didn't need psychic powers to know that; it was apparent from her eyes, and the way she held herself. But further to that, as soon as the reading began, a young girl came through, clear as glass. She said that she was Angie's daughter. As usual, at first I could only hear her initials, and then quickly after that made out her name. The spirit always comes through slowly at first. And since it is sounds that I hear, I sometimes get like-sounding names confused, and have to ask the client's help. Sally Anne told me that she had passed away at fourteen, and that it was something to do with her brain which killed her. She spoke of pain, but also, said that she was much happier now, and that she was no longer suffering.

She said that she wanted her mother to be happy too,

and to know that she was safe and well there. She was also attending college. Her mother seemed a little surprised by this; I think such a notion was quite alien to her understanding of the afterlife. But Sally Anne kept saying to me 'Tell her I'm training to look after children.' At that point I think Angie realized what I was saying must be true because she said that her daughter had been exploring training courses for childcare for when she left school and that from the earliest age she had wanted to be a nanny.

Sally Anne told me the names of her sisters, Ebony and Natalie, and knew what they were up to. She then started to tell me that she had met Paul. Her mother looked bewildered at this. 'Paul's her father, and he's still very much with us,' she said. But Sally was saying, 'No, not Daddy.' There was another Paul, who was twenty-one. Then it clicked. Sally Anne's father had been married before he met Angie. They had had a child, a little boy who had passed over when he was only two years old, suffering from whooping cough. And that was nineteen years ago. Paul was Sally Anne's half brother! I feel that this proves two things: first, that we grow up in spirit, reaching the age of twenty-one; second, that we meet up with those who know us or are connected to us.

Sally Anne also told me in another reading that Angie had recently got married. I had had no idea that she was not married to Sally Anne's father: they had been together for eighteen years, but they only recently decided to marry each other. 'She was at your wedding,' I said. 'She's telling me to tell you to look at your photographs.' 'I know,' said Angie. 'I've seen her in the pictures.' And indeed when she came back for another reading, she brought the wedding photos with her. There was a grey, ghostly form to be seen behind the married couple. This happens because of the energy radiated by the spirit, which the mechanical camera and its sensitive film can detect, even if the naked eye cannot.

Not all spirits make it into the spirit world, however. Some spirits are unable to ascend, and spend time roaming the earth plane instead. This can happen for a number of reasons. It can be a result of an untimely death. Should someone die suddenly and unexpectedly, not in the way they were destined to, then it may be that the spirits are not there waiting to collect them. The journey to the spirit world is a long one, and not everyone is able to find the way. Spirits are there to guide us in the right direction when we die. This is, according to Grandma Alice, what happened to old Mr Hughes, whose spirit I saw on the bridge when I was a child.

More recently, a neighbour who lived across the road called me on the phone.

'Who is that pretty young woman who's been standing at the gate at the end of your drive?' she asked. 'She's wearing a raincoat, and I've seen her there in all weathers.'

To be honest, I think she thought Mo had some girl who used to come calling for him! But from her tone of voice, I felt sure this was a spirit – although it is extremely unusual for a person who is not a medium or known to the spirit to see it so clearly. I told my neighbour I would go out and see.

As a precaution, I took the dog with me. They are terrified of spirits, and even if I didn't see anything, the dog's reaction would give me a pretty good idea if something was there or not. Sure enough, a few steps down the drive the dog shot back into the house. I couldn't see anything myself, however. I went down to the gate and up to the edge of the road to be sure.

When I came back into the house, the phone was ringing. It was my neighbour again. She sounded more than a bit shocked. 'You walked right through her!' she said.

I knew this girl must be waiting for someone, and the next day it all began to make sense. A lady came to see me who had recently lost her daughter, Jeanette, who had been in her early twenties. Jeanette had suffered from depression, and it had become so unbearable for her that sadly she had taken her own life. When the mother described her, and how beautiful she was, I knew that this was the girl my neighbour had seen – Jeanette had known her mother was coming to find me. During her mother's reading, Jeanette told me that her mother was going on to see people who were twins the next day, and that she was going to give them a present. And indeed, those were her plans.

In other cases it may be that spirits refuse to ascend because they are here guarding something or someone. This is most probably the reasoning behind the earthbound spirit at Doe Lea, who was watching over her child. Earthbound spirits manifest their presence in a number of ways, and even a lay person may be able to sense the presence of an earthbound spirit. They usually show themselves by moving objects round the house, interfering with electrical goods, switching lights on and off, or by causing a great deal of noise. It's their way of getting attention.

This all might sound rather alarming, but it is actually very easy to exorcize a spirit from the earth plane and send it in the right direction. A medium can rid a house or person of such a spirit simply by calling on other spirits or their spiritual guides to come and fetch that wayward or unruly spirit. Peace is then restored.

There are two types of earthbound spirits – those who are housebound and those who attach themselves to an individual, the most common type being those who attach themselves to a house or place. Rose was an old friend who moved nearby and whose life was turned upside down by the presence of a housebound spirit. She called me one day from her new house and told me that she was having problems. 'Something very strange is going on here,' she said. 'The taps keep turning themselves on, the doors are locking themselves, yesterday the tools got locked in the boot of the car, and there are leaks everywhere.' She asked if I could help, so I went to visit the house. It was a large, old building. When we entered the hall I could feel someone behind me, and I felt a chill down my neck. Instinctively, I headed for the downstairs bedroom, and as soon as I opened the door I saw in front of me the form of an elderly man, dressed quite shabbily. Almost at once a mist formed and he seemed to disappear. I went to the window and saw that he was now in the garden, standing directly in front of me. It was as if he had passed through the wall. Out loud, I asked him who he was.

'I'm the gardener,' he replied.

'Where are you?' I asked.

'I'm still here,' he said. 'I didn't know where to go.'

'I can help you,' I told him, 'but first you must tell me why are you causing so much distress to these people. They have never done anything to harm you.'

'Yes they have,' he retorted. 'It's the lady of the house. She's cut down the apple trees.'

I asked Rose if this was true. She looked surprised and said yes, they had cut them down to make a clearing. The spirit went on to tell me that he had lived in an old air-raid shelter in the garden. Rose looked confused; she didn't think they had one. But when we explored the garden later we managed to unearth one in the brambles and ivy.

The spirit told me he had succumbed to a fatal stroke and been buried in a pauper's grave. He had nothing, and had never known any family – which was probably why he was still here with us. No one had come to fetch him. I told him that he must leave these people and the house and ascend at once. He promised to do so.

But when I got home that evening I found that he was still with me. I could hear him, feel him. I called a friend, Jean, who is also a medium, and whom I had got to know when she bought a house nearby, as I felt that I needed some help. We prayed for the spirit and felt his presence leave. But that night I suffered another minor stroke, as though he had left his illness with me. Rose telephoned me the next day to say that everything was back to normal, and that peace had been restored. Thankfully, I too recovered.

Spirits who attach themselves to people are more sinister because they tend to pick on quite vulnerable types, and feed off their auras. I will explain this further later on. In some cases they might only be with that person for a number of hours, but in others an involuntary possession can take place, rendering the person who has been possessed feeling as though they have a dual personality, and that they are no longer in control of their thoughts or actions.

I read a possessed woman when I was running the guest house in Skegness. From the moment she entered the room I could sense that she was with a spirit. Her eyes were haunted, her smile tight, her hair dishevelled. Initially, she looked sad, but her expression quickly changed into that of a crazed person. I really didn't want to read her; she scared me, and I had never dealt with a possession before. But she was pleading with me for help. I asked her if there was anything wrong with her house. She said yes, but that it only happened in the bedroom.

'When I get in to bed it starts to move, it goes up and

down,' she said, 'but that's not why I've come. You see, he's perfectly friendly.'

Just the mention of the word 'he' sent a shiver down my spine. The spirit of a man was clinging to this vulnerable woman. As the reading went on it became clear what was going on. The spirit who had taken possession of this woman had, during his own lifetime raped and murdered a young girl in this bedroom. When he died, no one wanted to fetch him, so he remained earthbound, living his own hell, and had stolen this woman's mind. She began to cry, and confessed that she had started to do terrible things to her husband. She had reported him to the tax office, and even poured boiling fat over his naked body. 'I don't know why I am doing this. I do love him,' she wept.

I realized then that I was completely out of my depth with this case. I asked the spirit to leave, but he wouldn't go. I agreed to see her husband in a vain attempt to sort the mess out. He was exasperated by it all. 'This isn't the woman I married,' he kept saying. In his eyes, she had gone mad. I told him that the only things he could do were to lock her out of the house, however impractical that might seem, and keep her from that bedroom. But I learned later that when he did that she just broke the door down.

She came to me again, saying she felt better, and asked

for a reading. But I refused. I was overwhelmed with the most immense sense of foreboding as soon as she entered the room – the spirit was still with her. She asked me if we could have a private chat. Could we go and sit in her car? She was fumbling in her bag. All the time I kept hearing the voice of the spirit saying over and over again, 'I'm not afraid of you.' Then in my head I saw the image of a knife – she had a knife in her bag and she wanted to kill me. I shouted for help and got her out of the house as quickly as I could. I never heard from her nor, because they were together, the other spirit in her, again.

Not all spirits who attach themselves to people or houses are unruly or bad. There are those who have simply just lost their way or, like old Mrs Granfield back in Mansfield, do not realize that they have passed away.

I had one extremely rare case of a child who would not ascend. A woman had come to see me a couple of years before because she had lost her daughter. The child, who was four years old, had been killed suddenly in an accident. I used to dread this woman's readings, because I knew the child had not ascended. She had stayed on the earth plane because she had not been fetched, and she didn't realize that she had passed over. When the woman came for a reading I would not get her child in spirit as normally, for she still came with her mother. She would even appear on the sofa sitting next to her. And what was awful is that, unlike other spirit children, I could not say with confidence that she was happy.

'Tell Mummy I'm here,' she would say. She kept asking why her mother had put her toys away, or why wasn't she brushing her hair in the morning. 'Please do my hair,' she would say, 'it's blonde.' Then on one visit the mother said, as she was leaving, 'You know, Rita, a very strange thing happened to me the other night. I went to sleep as normal but when I woke up I found a hairbrush in my hand. I don't know how it got there.' In my mind I kept asking the girl's spirits to come and collect her and take her safely on. Eventually, I managed to get the woman's grandfather. When he came through I asked him to take the girl with him. I was able to make the spirit of the child appear in front of her mother and at the end I said, as I do with such transfigurations, 'Now you must go.' And with that she went, for when I came round from the transfiguration her apparition was gone.

The next reading with her mother was wonderful. The child was in spirit and was happy and safe.

But there doesn't necessarily have to be an emotional or physical bond between the person who has passed away and the living person for a spirit to remain earthbound. I once had a telephone call from a young woman who was very eager for an appointment. She told me that it was extremely important, and that she hoped that she might be able to see me that day. Normally, she would have been disappointed as I tend to be booked months in advance, but it just so happened that only minutes before she called someone had telephoned with a cancellation, so I agreed to see her that afternoon. The young woman was an air hostess, and was in between flights when I saw her for the appointment. When she walked into my reading room the first thing that she said was that she was not really sure why she was there.

'I've never been to a medium before, and I don't really believe in it, so I'm not sure why I've come all this way. I have no dead relations or friends, and I'm not interested in knowing my fortune,' she told me. 'But when I woke up this morning I kept thinking I must see a medium, I must, and I haven't been able to think about anything else all day.'

Given that the woman did not usually believe in what I could offer, and that she had travelled so far to see me, albeit on some strange impulse, one might have hoped that the reading would be a success, if only to prove a point. It wasn't. Halfway through it I remember thinking that I had never had so much difficulty with a reading for years. It wasn't that I couldn't pick up anyone in spirit who wanted to talk to her; on the contrary, I had quite a few spirits eager to speak, and the messages were loud and clear. The only problem being that they did not seem to be for her. 'I'm terribly sorry,' she said, 'but I just haven't got a clue about anyone you've mentioned.' It was quite apparent that the messages I was receiving bore no relation whatsoever to the life of this young woman. I was at a loss for words, and as confused as she was. Suddenly I felt the presence of an elderly man there with us, in my reading room.

'Has anyone passed away recently whom you might have had some contact with?' I asked her.

'No one I know personally,' she said, 'but on my flight yesterday a man I had been looking after died.'

She had been serving drinks and food on a long-haul flight to an elderly man sitting in an aisle seat. During the flight he fell asleep, and she put a blanket over him. When they were coming in to land in England, she noticed that he was still asleep, and she went to wake him so that she could adjust his seat into the landing position. But there was no response. She tried again, but still nothing. She realized that he had passed over. When they landed, the doctor said that the man had simply died of a heart attack.

The air hostess telephoned the airline while she was still at my house to find out more about this man. They told her his name, as well as those of his next of kin whom they had already contacted. She rang them herself, and found out some more information about the man and his life. Suddenly all the names I had mentioned to her fell into place, and it became obvious to us both that the reading I had given her was not meant for her, but for the dead man. The spirit of the man had seemingly attached himself to the woman because he did not know where to go. He had passed away so suddenly and between two places that his spirit was essentially lost, and so it linked itself to the first person that made contact with him. He had then brought this woman to me, so that through my connections with the spirit world, he would be able to free himself from her and ascend. The messages that I had received during the reading seemed to indicate that he wanted her to contact his relatives and let them know what had happened. Had she not come to me, or a medium who was able to exorcise it, the spirit might have stayed with her for some time. As it was, I was able to send him on his way, calling on his spirit guides to come and fetch him. The air hostess returned to London that afternoon, this time on her own.

Six

THE BOND THAT NEVER DIES

JUST BECAUSE a person whom we have known and loved in this life has passed over into the spirit world does not mean that the bond between us dies as well. Often it becomes stronger and more intense, for we tend to cherish the relationship we have known, holding and clinging on to it through our memories and recollections. 'All I have left of that person is my memories,' is a refrain I often hear when I am reading. When we lose a loved one it is usual for us to reconstruct the past. Hours can be spent looking through photograph albums, their former possessions, talking to friends and family about them, what they said, what they did, how they were special to us. That person's past becomes very important, and we become fearful of losing any of it, of forgetting.

But we should not just look at the past when we are thinking about that person. They are still very much with us. The relationship, the bond between us, carries on well past the grave. Relationships may manifest themselves in this life in physical terms, but their essence is the spiritual and emotional bond between two individuals. Many people suffering from grief long for their loved one to be back with them, asking why they left, saying, 'If only you were here now, if only for this moment . . .' But the spirits are always with us, still caring and loving just as much as they did when they were alive. The only difference is that we cannot see, hear or touch them. There are so many things that are beyond the reach of our five bodily senses; we just have to trust that they are there.

Some people who have been bereaved experience moments when they feel again the presence of the person who has passed away. For many it is just simply a gut feeling; a normal, everyday experience may be interrupted for a second or two by the notion that they are not alone. For no apparent reason they are made aware of the person they have lost, even though their mind is quite elsewhere, and there has been nothing in what they were doing at that moment to trigger a reminder or recollection. It is a warm feeling of love and happiness, quite different from anything else they may have experienced during the grieving process. And just as suddenly as it came, it goes again. In situations like this I believe the spirit is letting you know that they are with you and caring for you as you go about your life. They want you to know that you are not alone.

Grandma Mary Alice Thompson, with whom I spent so
much time when I was young. It was from her that I received
the gift. This photograph was taken long before I was born,
when she was 18, but even from a picture you can get
a sense of her striking presence.

Right
Me at the age of 24 with Pat aged 7 (left) and Julie aged 5 (right).

Below
Three generations of us on an outing. *Back row, left to right*: my mother, Dennis, Dad, me. *Front row*: my brother Steven, Mandy and Julie.

Above
On holiday with Mo on the island
of Jersey, where we have enjoyed
many summers.

Left
Kerry, my youngest, when she was five.

Standing on the pathway leading up to the front door of Ash House, where my grandmother said I would live. Next door are the ruins of a chapel. LESLEY HOWLING

Above
This is the chair I sit in when I am reading. The client sits on the sofa facing me, the bay window to their left. LESLEY HOWLING

Right
The walls of my reading room are covered with pictures of my 'spirit children', which have been given to me by their parents. Everyone comments on how warm and happy they make the room feel. LESLEY HOWLING

Ryan, whose parents came to see me all the way from South Africa. His mother had read about my work in my first book, *Reaching for the Children*.

Paul, who watches over his parents, David and Eileen.

Beautiful little **Lara**, who has become a great family friend.

Emma and Laura When I transfigured for their mother, Sandra, both girls appeared together. I believe they look after each other.

My grandmother's crystal ball. I don't actually use it in
my readings, but it is hundreds of years old, and a link to
my Romany past. LESLEY HOWLING

With Mo in our sitting room, Spring 1997. The window
looks out over the patio to the garden and field beyond.

LESLEY HOWLING

In other cases the experience may be more intense. Lara's mother, Beverly, said that even before she visited me she sensed that Lara was with her. She had been on the telephone to a friend one day when she felt as though she was being hugged very gently, as though her daughter had wrapped her arms around her. Other people tell me of things that have been moved around the house, or lights being turned on and off, of objects that may have been lost for years suddenly turning up. All these occurrences are the spirits' way of communicating with us, of letting us know that we should stop worrying, or feeling lost and alone. They are with us at all times.

Rick and Sue were a devoted, loving couple who worked together, running a chain of bookshops in the West Country. They had been married for thirteen years when, in December 1995, Rick passed away. Sue had arrived back home from work one evening and had gone to put her car away in the garage. As she opened the garage door she heard the noise of an engine running. To her horror, she found their delivery van with a pipe leading from the exhaust over to the passenger window. Clothes were stuffed into the windows. Rick had taken his life. He had left a note for Sue, explaining that he didn't want their relationship to end and that he still loved her.

Sue couldn't make any sense of what had happened. As a couple, they had enjoyed a happy and loving relationship, and could want for little more. In the months before Rick's passing, however, he had become withdrawn and subdued. But not for one moment had Sue sensed that he might take his own life. Unable to come to terms with what had happened, she eventually came to see me, and through the reading we were able to get a clearer picture of what had driven Rick to take his own life. This information, which has subsequently been backed up with further evidence that Sue stumbled on herself, was not the only positive thing that came out of her reading, as you will see. This story shows the incredible bond that still exists between a couple, even though one has passed away. It is as though Rick is always there for Sue, still looking after her in the way that he did when he was still alive. He seems to be aware of the fact that she is on her own, coping with both their business and her personal life, and he watches out for her. Sue has written this story in her own words.

SUE

I had only gone to Rita because my stepfather suggested it. Mediums were not really my kind of thing and I had been determined to cope with my grief in the conventional manner. But my stepfather said that she was good; he had gone to see her after the death of his first wife, and told me that her readings had been a great source of comfort. I suppose he could see my suffering, the fact that I could neither explain nor understand why Rick had taken his own life, and had not been able to help. Anyway, I made an appointment to see her, but did not think that much would come from it.

I remember the reading most vividly because Rita's very first words to me were, 'He loves you very much.' You can imagine how this made me feel. She had no idea of what had happened, that I had lost a husband, the way he had died. His suicide had naturally made me reflect on our relationship, on whether he did actually love me. I think this is a common reaction to suicide.

Rita described our shops to me, and told me how they were doing. She then said that 'Number Nine' should be sold. We did have a shop which we called 'Number Nine', so I was surprised by this information. She also told me that one of our pet dogs was ill and was not being treated properly. Later, when I got home, I looked at the figures for shop 'Number

Nine' and found it was not doing at all well; it was losing a lot of money and it was quite obvious from the books that it should indeed be sold. The following day I took the dog to a vet and found that it had a skin allergy and needed specialist treatment.

Rita told me that Rick had taken his life because he was being blackmailed by a woman. She described the place where this woman lived, a flat, and said that she had pestered him to the point where he couldn't cope with it any longer. She told me that my husband had not actually been having an affair with this woman, but that he was worried that if he stopped paying her money she would come to me and say that they were. Rick was not the type to stray, but I think he was terrified that had she told me they were involved I might leave him. I have looked into this since. I found the woman Rita had mentioned to me, who lives in a place which matches the description of the flat Rita had spoken of. I looked into our bank account and discovered that large sums of money had been withdrawn during the months before Rick's death. Had Rick continued to make these payments to this woman we would have suffered financially: he was in a no-win situation.

What I learnt from Rita, and what I subsequently was able to back up myself, certainly helped me. At first I felt vengeful toward this woman for driving my husband to his death, but I don't any more. I believe that in the long run she will get what is due to her. For me it became not so much a quest for *vengeance but to find out the truth. Rita helped me get this, but she also gave me something else, something more important. This is the knowledge and the proof that Rick is still with me. You see, the night before a reading I will talk to Rick and say what is worrying me, or how I feel. And invariably during the reading, without even prompting Rita, she will bring all these things up.*

On my second reading with Rita she came out with his name. Not an initial, not Richard, but Rick. She couldn't have remembered me, since the first reading was many months before, but she came out with all the same information again. She told me how much he loved me, that he visited every day. She said that Rick was telling her that I was redecorating our house and that he was laughing about how much they were charging me for the job. I would normally have left this sort of thing to Rick, were he still with me! I had made plans to sell 'Number Nine', and Rita said that the lease would be handed over in July. It was.

I had tried very hard to get on with my life after Rick's death. I went to as many social events as possible and even went on holiday, but life was still hard. I had lost my confidence, and found it difficult to be myself. On one occasion I had been invited to a family party. I had somewhat neglected my appearance after his death, and decided that on this occasion I must try and make an effort. I bought myself a bright red outfit. Before the party I kept looking in the mirror to see if it suited me, unsure about the colour and the way I looked in it. On my next visit to Rita one of the first things she said to me was, 'He likes you in red!' It made me smile. I suppose these are small things that don't mean very much to anyone else, but they matter to me enormously because it is as if he is still here helping me.

The reason why there is still such a strong spiritual link between Rick and Sue is the love that they had for each other in this life. In my experience the spiritual bond gets stronger the more deeply the couple have been in love. Theirs was certainly a love that transcends the grave. They are what I call soul mates, two individuals who were meant, destined to be together, always.

Between two such individuals exists an immutable law of attraction. However different they may seem at face value, they share the same spiritual qualities. It is an attraction that goes beyond looks, age, sexuality, class or background. On meeting that person there is at once a link, a bond that cannot be broken. Most people end up meeting their soul mate in unusual circumstances. You are meant to be together, and fate, or your spirit guides, will do their best to ensure that a union takes place, however improbable the circumstances.

Each of us has a soul mate. There is someone out there

with whom we have some spiritual connection, whom we were destined to spend at least a part of our lives with. But whether we end up married to or living with that person, or indeed whether we meet them at all in this life, is another matter. You may be married all your life to someone without them actually being your soul mate. In some cases this is fine, but equally they may not be the right person for you. You may be aware of the identity of your soul mate, but because of circumstance never connect with them in the fullest sense in this life. But, whatever the situation, you shouldn't worry for whatever happens here, and even if you spend your whole life on your own, in spirit you will be united with your soul mate. A husband and wife who were joined only by a legal tie in this life, between whom no love existed and who were in effect mentally divorced from one another, will no longer be together in the spirit world. They will each be united with another. Whether they knew them or not in this life is irrelevant. What matters is the fact that these two were always supposed to be together.

People often ask me who will be the soul mate of a person who has been married several times. I think in these situations the people really know themselves. It will be the one whom they really clicked with, the one who was their friend, the one they felt comfortable with. Soul mates are the people with whom we can really be ourselves. You may have several relationships in your life and have a great many friends and colleagues, but there are in fact only a very small number of people who really understand you, who take and like you as you are. Between you there is a spiritual bond. You don't have to have a romantic or physical relationship; the bond will still be there. It is possible to have more than one soul mate. There are instances, for example, where a person has lost the love of their life but later finds love with another. If you have loved two people equally in this life then you will go to them both in the next. As there is no jealousy in spirit, being with two people does not prove to be problematic. But if you didn't really love either of them, then you will not be with them. You only go where love is.

Those who have found their soul mate in this life but lose them to the next should not worry about 'remarriage' with another. As there is no sexual or emotional jealousy in spirit life, the one who has passed over won't feel hurt or envious of such a union. In most cases the spirit is happy with the knowledge that you are no longer on your own and that you are being cared for and loved as you deserve to be. Spirits hate to think of us as miserable and lonely; they want us to live with our lives as we need, but safe in the knowledge that we will one day be reunited.

Your meeting or romance with a new partner may even be as a direct result of their own spiritual intervention! I often hear in my readings that a spirit is pleased by their partner's remarriage. The only time they will voice an objection to a new relationship is if they feel that the union will be harmful to you, if the person is genuinely undesirable and is going to hurt or use you.

The bond between soul mates never diminishes but continues to grow. I can usually tell whether the person I am reading for has lost their soul mate within seconds. As the spirit comes through and starts speaking there is an immense feeling of love surrounding them. I once did a telephone reading for a woman in Wales called Rosemary. She was madly in love with her husband. They had known the deepest love and she was naturally devastated when he passed away. In the reading he came through, at once, very clear and strong. He told me he was protecting her in spirit, watching over her. He said, for example, that she should be careful as she had a hole in her roof, which she subsequently told me that she did have. He told her that he adored her and would never stop loving her. Rosemary, overcome with emotion, said back, 'God, I feel so close to you now.' At that moment, as clear as glass, we both heard him say in a strong male voice that was undoubtedly his, 'I love you.' That's all he said, but it was enough. Rosemary couldn't say anything more, and I too was dumbfounded.

It was one of the most beautiful things that I have ever witnessed in my work as a medium.

The spiritual link that I am discussing here doesn't only exist between those who have been in love. I find it is there between parents and children and brothers and sisters as well, particularly strongly in the case of twins. Twins are spiritually linked from conception, and much has been written and observed about the bond that exists between them while they are alive and growing up. There are countless stories about how twins who have been separated at birth still manage somehow to lead parallel lives. Some twins say they experience the sensation of pain when the other has been hurt. Others talk of a psychic bond that exists between them, that one knows when something bad has happened to the other, for example.

Again, the bond that exists between twins, like the one that links soul mates, transcends death. The tie that binds these two individuals does not diminish when one passes over before the other. Their link is incredibly strong. I find twins' readings quite astounding because they tend to be so clear and accurate. The details one will give on the other's life tend to be very precise, as though they have been there at all times, living the other's life. In my experience this tends to happen when a twin dies too. The spirit of the twin who has passed away will ascend as usual, but although not earthbound will spend as much time on the earth plane with their living twin as possible, to watch and guide them.

Matthew and James were identical twins. When Sally, their mother, gave birth to them she was over the moon. Not one, but two, perfect babies. They had been born prematurely but they were being taken care of and seemed healthy enough; the doctors said there was nothing to fear. But Sally's joy was to be short-lived. Three weeks after his birth Matthew passed away.

Sally never really got over the loss of her son. Many of her friends told her not to worry, that at least she had James. Whilst Sally realized that they meant well, telling a mother who has lost her baby not to worry because she had more doesn't help to heal the wound. The fact was that she had known a life, albeit briefly, and now it had been taken from her. James was not a substitute for Matthew, he was a child in his own right. He grew up, made a success of his life, getting a good job, marrying and started a family. Sally has always adored James, but she knew from the moment she was told that her baby had died she would spend the rest of her life missing Matthew.

By his mid-twenties, James was married. Seven years

ago his wife, Catherine, telephoned Sally to say that she was having problems with the house. Strange things had been happening. It started with small pieces of furniture which kept moving around. There was a great deal of banging at night and the lights kept turning on and off. Then clocks and the television went haywire. Sally was concerned for Catherine, especially since she was pregnant, but Catherine told her not to fret. She said that neither she or James were alarmed by what was going on. She said that however peculiar it all was, for some reason they weren't frightened by any of it. Sally immediately thought that it must be Matthew, that he was trying to communicate with his twin.

Although Sally thought this, she would have left the matter alone had she not come across a letter that she had received a fortnight before. It was from distant relatives that she had not seen for some time. They had lost a grand-daughter recently, and they spoke of this in the letter. At the end of the note they had written down a telephone number. There was nothing next to it. No explanation, no name, just a number. Sally thought nothing of it at the time, but after her conversation with Catherine she suddenly felt compelled to dial the number. She had no idea who she was calling, but she did it anyway. When I answered the telephone she asked me who I was.

When I told her what I did she made an appointment

to see me, but I knew nothing about her life or family. As soon as she set foot in the reading room I felt Matthew there, and told Sally. I said to her that I felt that he was with them all a great deal, and that he spent a lot of time with his twin. He told me James's name and all about Catherine. He said that he had been with them at their wedding and that he had walked up the aisle with them. He told me that he had created havoc in James's house because he was excited about the birth of their first child. He said the word 'Bosch', so I realized that one of the ways he must be trying to let them know he was there was by messing around with the electrical appliances.

It seems Matthew has never left his brother's side. He remains on the earth plane at all times so that he can look after James. He told me that during one of James's job interviews he was there. Sally confirmed that electrical equipment in the office had started to play up, and an object had moved on the desk. He wanted his brother to get the job, so he came to the interview with him. It is as though he is always guiding him, pointing him in the right direction. James talks about having a great instinct about people, which is probably Matthew telling him who to trust and who to be wary of.

On another occasion James and Catherine, who was pregnant at the time, were driven off the road by a juggernaut. Their car was a write-off, but to everyone's surprise, James, Catherine and her unborn baby walked away from the accident without even so much as a cut.

When James's and Catherine's first child, Luke, was born, Matthew was there. Sally was astounded by the resemblance between her grandchild and her own twins when they were born. As Luke grew older too it was as though Matthew was with him twenty-four hours a day and even that he was showing himself to the child. Luke would often say things like, 'Daddy home,' or 'Daddy in garden,' when in fact James was away on a business trip. One night when Sally's daughter, Emma, was reading *Peter Pan* to Luke at bedtime she asked him if he would like to fly. He replied that he *did* fly, every night, with Uncle Matthew. The dimmer lights in his bedroom were always going up and down, and the window kept opening and shutting seemingly of its own accord. When Dominic, their second child, was six, his parents asked him one day what he was laughing so hysterically about. 'It's Uncle Matthew. He's jumping up and down on that van!' he said.

It is normal for a twin to be around the one who has survived and for them to feel that link, but what is interesting in this case is that Matthew seems to want to be with his family, and in particular around his brother and his sons, all the time. It is as though he has chosen to be here with his family rather than be fully in spirit.

Matthew will probably remain on this plane acting as his brother's guardian angel until the time when James passes away, at which point his twin will ascend, his work over.

The spiritual bond is especially strong between children and parents who have outlived them. Every passing is difficult to cope with and understand, but in my experience the grief suffered by a parent who has lost a child seems to know no bounds. It is a wrench like no other. Even if one does believe in an afterlife, such a loss is almost too difficult to bear. There seems to be no justice, no rhyme or reason to it, and as in so many cases I have seen, it often leaves the parent feeling suicidal.

The bond between the spirit child and parent is strong because it is one that in this life has been cut short. And whilst that child is cared for in spirit by others there, I find that the child likes to visit their family throughout the day and grow there with them, too. They will be there at family events and occasions. They follow their parents everywhere, and will go out of their way to let them know that they are with them always.

Paul, who passed away when he was only nineteen, spends a great deal of time with his family, especially with his heartbroken father, David. Their bond is particularly intense. Paul often comes to David in dreams. Here David tells his story in his own words.

PAUL

When Paul passed away, my wife Eileen and I found it difficult to cope. We didn't know that such suffering was possible. We wanted to find someone we could talk to about what was going on and how we felt about our loss. We had been to mediums in the past but felt none of them was genuine; we just knew that they weren't really talking to our son. Rita had been recommended to us by a cousin of ours, and although she said she was good, I remember feeling very nervous about the whole thing. I couldn't take another disappointment – it is very hard when you have lost someone to keep seeing people who cannot come up with anything. You begin to lose hope, and start to despair. You want to believe that there is an afterlife, but how can you when someone gets it all so wrong?

By the time I went to see Rita, I was very depressed. I simply didn't want to live any more. But I was also desperate to find an affirmation of what I believed in deep down. For, whilst Paul was no longer alive, we felt that he was still with us.

Paul was our only natural child. We have a lovely, beautiful daughter, Elizabeth, whom we adopted, but when Paul died I felt as though we had been robbed of something that we had fought so hard for. Paul, you see, suffered from cystic fibrosis. When he was born he had only a 10 per cent lung capacity. We were told that he probably wouldn't live for more than six months, but he proved them all wrong. They said that he wouldn't make six. Again, he defied them, reaching the age of nineteen. He was a wonderful, determined boy who fought against all the odds. He lived a full and normal life, passing his driving test first time and finding his vocation as an excellent cook, taking great pride in what he did. Even from when he was quite young, every year he would make our family Christmas cake.

Despite our anxiety about meeting Rita, the reading could not have gone better. As soon as we entered Rita's house we found an inner peace. Rita got Paul's name straight away — and she didn't know us, or anything about our lives. She had never set foot in our house, but there she was describing it, describing Paul's bedroom, telling me exactly what clothes we had buried him in. Rita talked about things that only we could have known about, small details that made us realize she had indeed got Paul with her. She told us, for example, that Paul had said a tape cassette was missing from his room. We didn't know what she was talking about. We had left our son's room exactly as it was, hadn't removed anything from it. But later when we went home I was telling Elizabeth about the reading, and mentioned this in passing. Elizabeth said that she had borrowed a tape of his to record. We couldn't believe it. Rita mentioned that a vase had been moved from the window ledge in his bedroom. She was right. My wife had moved it days before. It was this kind of information which made us realize that Paul had not left us at all. He would never leave us. This changed our lives.

Now we know that Paul is around us the whole time, at family events, at mealtimes. He is often quite mischievous and likes to play jokes on people. He visits Rita a great deal and gets her to pass on messages to us. Most of the time they don't make any sense to her, but we always know what he is talking about.

I have become much more spiritually aware since his passing. I think I have learnt to look at life in a different way. When I suffered from a heart attack I had my own near-death experience, as if my son was showing me something. I remember feeling as though I was trapped in a tin of sardines, for the darkness rolled back as I lay there and a light shone in on where I was. I heard a voice say, 'We've got him'. I felt happy. I wanted so much to go through that opening toward the light, to be with my son. But Paul didn't want me to yet, and I felt a surge of warmth as I came back. Since then I believe that he shows himself to us as if to say, 'You didn't have to die to be with me, because I am always with you.'

A couple of days before I went to see Rita for a further

reading, Paul came to me. I was awake when it happened, but it felt like a dream. He was with a girl who had long, curly blonde hair and bright blue eyes. She told me that her name was Alison. They were holding hands. Rita later described the same girl to me, the piercing eyes, the hair. I had not said anything to Rita about what had happened. Rita told me that she was Paul's girlfriend, that he had found his soul mate in the spirit world.

Every time we see Rita, Paul will tell us what we have been doing since our last visit. He will know that we have been to the cemetery, for example, or that we were with friends at the weekend. He will repeat what I may have said in the car afterwards. Rita knew, for example, that I had a heart attack, because Paul had told her. She knew it was his birthday when we visited her. No one could just come out with that kind of thing, it is so personal. These are small things, silly details, jokes, remarks about my socks or something like that, even the way she recounts things, but they all act as proof that Paul is with us still, living and growing. It is as though he never left.

Seven

WHEN A SPIRIT SHOWS ITSELF

TRANSFIGURATION IS the process by which a spirit shows itself to those on the earth plane. It is sometimes referred to as 'materialization'. Whilst there are a great many mediums with clairvoyant and clairaudient skills, transfiguration mediums, who have the ability to make a spirit materialize, are few and far between. It is possibly the rarest of all psychic phenomena, and it takes a great deal of patience, skill – and nerve – to master.

During a transfiguration the spirit entity manifests itself, building a temporary duplicate of its physical form, on to or near the body of the medium. Where transfiguration differs from apparition is that the spirit only shows itself at the request and will of the medium. As in clairaudience and clairvoyance, during a transfiguration the medium acts as a channel through which the spirit can show itself. The medium enters a state of self-induced possession, and calls on that spirit to come forward and be seen. What usually happens is that the spirit coming through will transpose its own image on to the face of the medium.

What you are seeing, therefore, is not the person themselves but an image of them. A transfiguration involves the use of a substance that mediums and spiritualists call ectoplasm which the transfiguration medium is able to generate. It is an almost invisible substance, a colourless, slightly cloudy, fluid, with a structure that allows it to manufacture an image of the human body. The spirit makes the fluid form into an image of itself. However, not all spirits are capable of being transfigured, so it cannot always work. Once they reach the spirit world, those who have passed over need to learn how to show themselves, which is why some come through more vividly than others. A spirit who has only just passed over or learned to show itself may not come through very well on first attempt.

If the medium is not fully focused on what he or she is trying to achieve, or is distracted by the slightest noise or movement around them, the transfiguration will not occur. The trance is so intense that the medium will be quite unaware of what has happened for minutes afterwards. For the medium it is like entering a deep sleep, and upon waking feeling dazed and unsure of where one is. The medium sees nothing during the transfiguration. His or her mind has switched off, their vision blurs, everything becomes hazy. Before they begin the process the medium will have inwardly asked the spirit to come forward and show itself to the person having the reading, and they will also remind the spirit that after it has done this it must leave the medium's body and return to the spirit world. A transfiguration should *only* be a vision. The spirit should not try and possess the medium! The process is extremely draining for the medium both physically and mentally, and many transfiguration mediums suffer from headaches afterwards.

What the client witnesses during a transfiguration can vary. Some transfigurations can last for quite long periods of time, but on other occasions the person may only have a glimpse of the spirit. Yet the process itself does not seem to change. The person having the sitting will be asked to stare into the eyes of the medium. Having made eye contact, they will notice that a mist gradually seems to form around the body and face of the medium. Everything will become a blur until all that they can see are the medium's eyes. Slowly the mist starts to clear and begins to take form. Features will begin to take shape around the face and shoulders. The process is gradual. The medium does not suddenly transform into the shape of another person. It is usual for the nose or mouth to form first. Sometimes only a couple of features will come through, but they are quite distinguishable and distinct from those of the medium. On other occasions the image will be extremely vivid and clear, and may cover the medium's entire body.

When Paul's father, David, came for his first transfiguration, he was understandably very nervous. He told me that he was worried because he thought if he saw Paul he would not want to let him go at the end of it. I assured him that this would not be the case and that once Paul had tried to come through, and if he had succeeded in doing so, he would leave of his own accord when he thought that David had seen enough. During the first transfiguration David did not see all of his son, but he said afterwards that he had seen enough to realize that it was Paul. He said that where my black hair would have been he saw mousey hair beginning to form. He could see the top of his head. He saw his nose form, my dark eyes change into those of his son. I asked him what it was like afterwards. 'I saw enough to know that it was Paul,' he said. The second time we attempted a transfiguration it was more successful. This time David saw all of Paul. He said that the mist which had formed in front of me seemed to clear bit by bit, and as it did so the image of Paul appeared upon my face. David admitted to me later that it had upset him, not because he was frightened but because he found it very moving. He said that it was a strangely comforting experience.

I would not advise everyone who comes through my door for a reading to have a transfiguration. It is an extremely personal and intense experience. Some people who are prepared to contact and communicate with their spirits are simply neither ready nor prepared for such an encounter. Moreover, for such a process to work, the person who has come for the reading must have a very strong link with a spirit. They do not necessarily have to have known the spirit, it could be an ancestor or your spirit guide who materializes, but the link must be strong enough for that spirit to want to show itself to you. Spirits are not just there to amuse us or to prove something to us. A transfiguration is not a performance. It is an intimate moment between a spirit who wants to be seen and a person who wants that spirit to show itself to them. They are not always successful either. It depends a great deal on how the medium feels, whether they are physically and mentally up to it, and the environment in which they are working. I have never been able to transfigurate, for example, in front of a crowd. This is not just because of the obvious distractions, but more to do with the fact that spirits do not want to come through to a whole group of strangers. They will only want to show themselves to those they love, care for, or watch over.

*

Though I was aware of my psychic abilities from an early age, I did not know that I was able to transfigurate spirits until much later on in life. The strange medium at Doe Lea had said that I had the gift, but back then I did not really understand what she was talking about, or, for that matter, really want to know. 'You're a transfiguration medium,' she had said after the events of that terrible night. 'That's very rare, you should use it.' To be quite honest, I had no real understanding of what transfiguration was all about. How could I use a talent I didn't understand? Who would teach me? I didn't think about it again for years and years. Then one day I stumbled across this gift quite by accident.

It was while I was running the guest house in Skegness. Like the story of my early life, this is an experience I discussed with John Man in *Reaching for the Children*, but it needs to be retold to put my growing understanding of this gift into context. It was 1985, and I had been reading for a woman called Anne who had lost her son in a road accident. Her son, Carl, was a picture-framer. He was eighteen. Anne had been driving back from her sister Jill's one night when she realized that the road into which she would have normally turned to get home was blocked. There were police everywhere. There must have been an accident, she thought to herself, but didn't think much more about it until an hour or so later when the police knocked at her door. Carl had been killed in a car accident they said, and it was the very one Anne had driven past that night.

Carl had gone out in Skegness that night with his friends, Roger, Chris and Nick. The car had veered off the road and had turned over on to the bonnet of an oncoming car. Three of them had been killed, only one had survived. All Anne could think about was whether her son had suffered – she needed to know. She had always believed that life was mapped out, but a death so young seemed senseless. A friend had recommended that she visit a medium who lived nearby in Cecil Avenue. Anne was too listless even to make an appointment, but her friend insisted that she go.

As soon as I set eyes on Anne, I could sense that something terrible had happened to her. You wouldn't have needed the gift to know that, she looked awful. It turned out that she hadn't eaten for weeks, or slept. As soon as I began to read for her I knew that she had lost someone, but sensed that it wasn't her husband, but someone much younger. I could feel a strong bond between her and the young male spirit who was coming through.

'It's your son, isn't it?' I said. She broke down, collapsing to her knees.

'Why did you leave me? Why? If only I could see you now,' she gasped.

I told Anne that whilst I was able to help her communicate with her son, I couldn't bring him back to her. I felt he was happy, warm and pleased that she had come. At that moment I started getting other names in my head. They came in quick succession.

'Who is Roger?' I asked. 'And Nick? And Chris?' In my head I saw there was a tree and a bridge involved. Carl told me that he had lost his watch.

Anne's tears dried, and she sat there in disbelief for even if I had researched her life or heard about the accident, this was one thing I couldn't possibly have known about. When the police had given her Carl's possessions, she had noticed that his watch was missing. Carl told me that he had taken it off just before the accident to change the time on it. It was still there in the wreckage, he said, under a mat. That was the last thing he remembered. The news relieved Anne. It meant that he had not suffered. He had died instantly, just as the police had told her. Then it all started to flow, things that meant nothing to me, but made a great deal of sense to Anne. How he loved to cook, that he dyed his blue shoes black after being teased about them by his friends. What Anne had removed from his bedroom since he had passed over. The names of his brothers and sisters. Her son was saying that she should stop crying; he had learnt that he was always destined to die young.

I read for Anne quite frequently after that. She seemed

to be coping with her grief a lot better every time I saw her. I watched her go through all the emotions of a parent struck down by all consuming grief. And while I may have helped her, she also helped me, because it was really through Anne that I realized that there was some purpose to my work. There was more to mediumship than fortune telling.

It was during Anne's fourth reading that it happened. Anne seemed to be staring into my eyes, and she remarked that during the reading my gaze seemed to intensify. The room seemed to obscure to the point where all she could do was focus on my face. She said that my face kept changing, and that it was scaring her. I was feeling quite odd myself by this point, such was the strength of Carl's presence. I was feeling claustrophobic, and it was as if the air in the room was getting thinner. 'I think that Carl is trying to come through to you,' I said. At that moment I looked up and saw him across the room, coming towards me. I felt a contraction in my solar plexus, my stomach turned, my vision blurred as if a mist was filling the space. I could no longer see Anne.

I came round within seconds. Anne had seen nothing, but then it started to happen all over again. Within five seconds it was over.

Anne sat there blinking with disbelief. 'I saw him!' she

said, almost in a whisper. She said that she had seen his image forming across my face, the very likeness of him. She was stunned. So was I!

The experience left me feeling physically drained, but I was excited by what had happened. It didn't scare me as I realized this was a gift I could use to help people. But I knew that I had to practise it a great deal, and learn to control it, if I was going to start seriously using it in my readings.

By this time my children were quite aware of my work, and Kerry even used to help me keep track of my appointments. So I was able to persuade my daughter, Mandy, to act as a guinea pig and allow me to practise on her. I thought that I might be able to transfigurate her father, Dennis, for her. I was not entirely sure of what to do, but as I always do when I read, I summoned my spirit guide, Running Water, to ask for his assistance. Mandy was naturally apprehensive, so I told her that if at any time during the process she was scared and wanted me to stop she should raise her arm.

The transfiguration was a success, but it wasn't Dennis who came through. Mandy told me afterwards, for I never have any recollection of what has gone on during the transfiguration, that I had entered a trance-like state, and had slumped back into my chair. A mist formed all around me until she could see nothing except my eyes. As the mist seemed to clear, my face appeared to have broadened. High cheek-bones had formed, my skin was dark and pitted, and my eyes were heavy-lidded, as though there was something wrong with them. She could see dark, shoulder-length hair, and on the top of my head there seemed to be some kind of headdress. I was speaking to Mandy during the transfiguration, although again I can't remember doing so, but she said my voice had changed. It was a masculine voice, deep and throaty, and I had a strange accent, one that she couldn't place. 'It just weren't you!' she said afterwards. And it wasn't me, it was my spirit guide, Running Water. The face Mandy had described matched the image I had seen of him on the eve of my marriage to Dennis. That was an experience I had never mentioned to any of my children.

During the transfiguration I apparently told Mandy that there was going to be an accident involving a red car: a head-on smash that would leave the headlights of the car hanging out from their wires. I told her not to worry because she wouldn't be hurt, but she was still extremely freaked by my premonition. Scared, she had wanted me to stop the transfiguration. She put her arm in the air as I had instructed her to do, but there had been no response from me. As with all the transfigurations that I have performed over the years I was simply not conscious of what was going on around me. It was only when she started to shout and scream, that I finally came round.

Mandy owned an old red Mini at the time, and didn't feel comfortable driving it from that afternoon onwards. She decided to sell it and so put an advertisement in the local paper. One evening a girl called round and asked if she could take the car for a test drive. She asked Mandy if she would go with her, but after the transfiguration Mandy didn't want anything to do with the car, so the girl went on her own. The girl took some time, and when she returned she was flustered. She had had an accident, and smashed the car against a tree. The girl was fine, but a bit shaken. We went out to see the damage to the car. It wasn't that bad, but its headlights were hanging out by their wires.

After that experience, I thought it best not to perform another transfiguration on Mandy. But the gift can be difficult to control and, unfortunately for Mandy, Running Water wasn't the only spirit who decided to show himself to her.

A couple of years ago I was sitting in my reading room giving a telephone reading to a woman called Connie when Mandy dropped round for a visit. Connie is a masseuse who lives in Las Vegas, and I have been reading her for a good many years now. In May 1987, Connie's only daughter, Rebecca, was tragically killed in another road accident. Rebecca was only seventeen and all her family and friends were devastated. Perhaps Rebecca possessed some psychic powers of her own, for it turned out she never did think that she would live beyond her eighteenth birthday. In the month before her passing she had told her mother how she dreamt one night that she had been killed in a car crash. Rebecca had also shared this dream and the belief that she would die soon with her friends. She had also asked them to wear pink at her funeral, for that was her favourite colour. Everything about Rebecca was pink, the wallpaper in her bedroom, the carpet, all her clothes.

I have a great affection for Rebecca. Whenever she comes through in a reading she is extremely lively and funny, and she can be quite cheeky too. I remember a time when Connie had travelled all the way from America to Derbyshire just to see me for a reading. The first thing she said to her mother was, 'You've got pink underwear on!' Connie blushed. She had! I have also spoken about Rebecca a great deal to my family, and they know all about her and her love of pink. So it was that as I was on the telephone to Connie that afternoon, Mandy came into the reading room with a sandwich and sat on the sofa opposite me. I wouldn't normally let someone else into the room during a reading, as it is such a private moment and I don't want any distractions, but the whole family knew Connie and Rebecca, and Connie didn't mind Mandy being there. Mandy was eating her sandwich and staring down at her feet. She had some new summer shoes on which were pink and flowery. 'I bet Rebecca would love these shoes,' she evidently thought to herself. At that moment Mandy looked up at me, and as I turned towards her she saw that my face had changed. My hair was long brown and curly, and I looked like a teenager. Mandy recognized Rebecca from a photograph I keep of her. And then evidently I spoke. 'Yes, Mandy, I do like your shoes.' Then I returned back to myself. But Mandy just sat there, having dropped her sandwich, and was staring at me with her mouth hanging open. Although she was usually very comfortable with the goings-on of the spirit world, I have never seen anyone turn so white in all my life.

What the transfiguration of Rebecca shows is that not only can spirits read our thoughts, but that they are able to show themselves to us when they choose to. They still need the medium to be able to do this, but they have their own will to decide when and where they appear even if they have not been summoned. On another occasion I was reading for a woman when her mother-in-law appeared. The woman had been visiting me for some time, but was having to come behind her husband's back since he didn't really approve of such things. On the day she came for her reading she was a bit late. She explained that this was because her husband had gone to the hospital for a check-up. It was nothing serious, which was why she had still kept her appointment. We had just begun the reading when an old woman appeared in the bay window of the reading room. We could both see her. She looked rather cross. 'Oh my God!' exclaimed the woman, 'It's my mother-in-law!' The mother-in-law had come because she wanted the woman to go to the hospital and be with her husband. So the woman left immediately, and went to her husband's side. She told me later that he had been diagnosed with Parkinson's Disease, and she was grateful that she could be there to support him.

When I am transfiguring, I cannot guarantee that the spirit who comes through is necessarily the one that the client wants to see. This is particularly true in cases where a recipient has lost more than one friend or family member to the spirit world. Sometimes one spirit might come after the other, but again this is dependent on whether the spirits are able to show themselves, and whether I am up to it. When Sandra came to see me for a reading, and I offered to transfigure for her, a very unusual thing occurred: two spirits actually came together. Half of one face, half of the other, appeared over mine at once. It was something that had never happened to me before or since.

Sandra lost her two granddaughters, Emma and Laura, six years ago in the most tragic of circumstances. Emma, who was four and half, and her sister Laura, two and half, had been left in the care of their other grandmother, whilst their parents, Nick and Helen, were out for the day. When they returned that afternoon there was nothing left of their home. A petrol bomb had been put through their letterbox, and the house had burnt to the ground. The children had died from asphyixiation, and Nick's mother, who was badly burned, was rushed to intensive care. The man responsible for this hideous crime is now serving two life sentences.

When Helen and her mother, Sandra, came to me, they were completely distraught. I hoped that their readings might offer them some kind of comfort during this terrible period of their lives.

Whenever I read for them, the girls would always come together. They were wonderful, happy children who liked to joke with their mother. They would say things that I did not understand, but when I repeated them to Helen she would just laugh, later explaining them to me. Once when Helen came for a reading alone, they told me that she was going to have a baby. I asked her if she was pregnant: she said that she didn't think so, but two weeks later she discovered that she was!

Despite all that had happened, these readings were very happy events because the girls were so lovely and funny, and also because there was the knowledge that they were not alone, but rather that they still had each other. This is why, I believe, Emma and Laura came together during Sandra's transfiguration. It was as if they were holding hands.

SANDRA

I had seen Rita on a couple of occasions since Emma and Laura passed away. As a family we had all suffered a great deal, and we all went through great lows. Visiting Rita eased that for me, her readings gave me some strength, and got me through some of the worst stages.

On one occasion after the girls had come through to Rita, she asked me if I would like to see them. I had never seen a transfiguration before, nor even thought about having one – the readings had always been so wonderful, and we would know from what Rita was saying that it was them. But that day I thought, 'Why not?' Rita did explain that they might not come through, and that if they did, she could not be sure which one would come.

It was daylight outside, but Rita pulled the curtain slightly across and asked me to concentrate on her eyes. I was sitting directly opposite her, and stared at her face. Gradually it began to alter. There was a slight haze in front of it to start with, but when that cleared I could actually see both girls! On one half of her face was Laura, on the other was Emma. They were quite distinct – and the girls were different to look at: Emma had an oval face like her father's, whereas Laura's was round. You could see this in the trasfiguration.

The experience only lasted a couple of minutes but it felt like longer. At the time I remember thinking to myself, 'Is this really happening?' The image was so vivid, but it defied all normal belief. When you have suffered the kind of loss we did, the desire to believe for the sake of solace can be extremely strong. I was very aware that I wanted to see them so badly that I could have convinced myself that I was seeing them even if I wasn't. But despite all this, I know what I saw that afternoon. However unbelievable it seemed then, or to others reading this, I knew that I had seen them and that I had not imagined it.

It was a very strange, intense experience. I am not sure it is right for everyone – people deal with these things in very different ways. But it gave me a feeling of comfort and strength.

Eight

THE FUTURE

FROM THE moment we are born, our lives are fated. Each life is predestined to follow a certain course. It seems our births, marriages, children, separations, disappointments and ultimately our deaths have already been determined by a greater force.

The concept of fate is alarming to some people because believing in it implies that there is no such thing as free will. We are not living our lives, they say, but simply fulfilling a role, puppets playing to the whims of a higher force. And therefore, if the course of our lives has already been determined, any idea that we have the will or the ability to change it, to make any difference, becomes fraudulent. We might as well become apathetic and indecisive, for if we are fated there are no real decisions to be made; we may as well sit back and watch the inevitable unfold. If there is nothing we can do to alter the course of events, what is the point of trying? We might as well just resign ourselves to what has been predetermined.

There is a degree of logic to this argument, but in my way of thinking it doesn't follow through. After all, we cannot give in to predestination, resigning ourselves to our fate, if we do not know what that fate is. Our lives may be a journey that has been mapped out for us, but we do not, as mortals, have access to the map. Furthermore, in my experience predestination doesn't affect every aspect of our lives. It merely serves as a blueprint for significant events. We may all be destined to arrive at a given place, but like any journey, there are a number of routes which we can take to get there, and it is up to the individual to find or choose the way. Thus we still have choice, reason and the ability to make our own decisions. Sometimes the path we take is not the best one. We may also get lost, or take a longer route than we should have done. Similarly, there will be times when, through luck or clear foresight, we arrive at our destination quickly, without confronting any problems along the way.

A young man might come for a reading and be told that his soul mate, the person he is destined to be with, has not yet come into his life. The medium, through communication with the man's spirit guides, describes this particular person and the circumstances in which the man will meet her. The medium predicts that they will marry. The man is confused and upset because he believes that he has already met his soul mate, but she does not fit the description he has been given by the medium. He is predestined to be with his soul mate, yet he consciously decides to ignore what the medium has said, and carries on with his current affair, living his life accordingly. And he is right to do so. For although his affair eventually ends, it ends up being through this relationship that he meets the woman the medium has described as his soul mate and he marries her. He chose to take his own path but ultimately, he arrived at his given destination. Remember, though, that we are only told what we need to hear. The spirit would not say this if the man's current good relationship would be threatened by knowing this – the spirit would know how the man would receive the news. But equally, if the man's current affair was for some reason unhealthy, and ought to end in order that the man could be free to meet his destined soul mate, or for that matter avoid preventable harm, the spirit would warn the man specifically about this.

It is only because there is such a system of predestination that a medium is able to prophesy to any degree what may happen in the future. Futurizing is this ability to predict what lies ahead for an individual. But this gift does rest with the medium, in that it is not the medium who is able to foretell future events. The act of prophecy lies with the spirit guides. As always, the medium only serves as a means of communicating these messages. When I tell a young woman that she will give birth to two sons, or a middle-aged man that he is about to change his career radically, these are not *my* prophecies but the words of their spirit guides. It would irresponsible for any living person to predict such events as we simply don't have access to this information. I wince at being called a fortune teller. The information must come from somewhere, from someone who knows the person concerned.

The spirit world is aware of what our fates are, and part of its role is to help us along that way. Because the spirits are around us day and night, they know what is going on, and because they are aware of our destinies, they know what will happen. They might warn you that the man you are seeing is not right for you, and so predict that he will make you very unhappy. They can do this because they have been with him, have seen what he is like when he is not with you, or even *who he is* with when he is not with you. The spirit guides are there to protect you, to steer you in the right direction. They do not, because they cannot interfere with what has ultimately been destined for you.

My grandmother said to me before she died, 'Whatever harm comes to you, I'll reverse it.' What she meant was that she would not stop things from happening to me, because they were fated to occur, but she would do her best to put them right. She could not prevent the death of my husband Dennis, for example, but she helped me through the hard times afterwards. In a reading a spirit may come and tell you of something that is about to happen in the future so that you can prepare for it, or so as to stop you from worrying about something, but they do so only to guide you. They don't interfere in what has already been determined. They cannot alter your whole destiny.

There seems to be a code of practice at work when it comes to futurizing. I have noticed, for example, that spirits do not like to futurize on financial matters. They will talk of money that is about to come your way, such as an inheritance, but they do not help you to play the stock market. The reason for this is that they will only talk of things that are destined. A pay rise, an insurance policy, money won through a court case, these may be predicted because the money was meant to come your way. That you are about to receive a large amount of money from your late uncle's estate is allowed because it has been determined. But they will not tell you the lucky lottery numbers because – unless you are fated to win, in which case you do not need to know the numbers anyway – it goes against what has been determined for you. Divine intervention on gambling matters would, I feel, alter the balance of life for the worse. There would be a great many lottery winners, but not enough money to hand out! My job is as a medium, not as a financial adviser. Mediumship can certainly be beneficial to business, and many business people consult mediums to find out what direction they should take, for a spirit may be able to advise that person that they should brave out a deal they are worried about, that they should be wary of the man who is sharing their desk, that it would be a mistake to fire an employee. They advise us in these matters just as they would in other areas of our lives, but they are not there to help us to get rich quick. If we do, then it is because we were always destined to do so.

Some people who come to see me, tell me at the beginning of their reading that they are not interested in hearing about the past or indeed what is happening currently in their lives. What they want to know about is the future. Will they marry? If so, to whom and when? Will they be rich? Will they get the job they have just applied for? I'm afraid such people will always be disappointed. I am not an oracle but a *medium*, and as such can only tell them what their spirit guides want them to know.

A young girl once telephoned me for a reading. Within minutes I had contacted the spirit of her late grandmother, a lively, warm lady who was keen to speak to her granddaughter. I told the girl this and named her grandmother, but she just didn't want to know. 'Oh, I'm not interested in talking to *her*,' she snapped. 'I want you to tell me about my relationship, whether I should stick with my boyfriend or leave him for this other chap.' Had the girl bothered to communicate with her grandmother, she might have got her answer. As it was, the spirit was made unwelcome, and the reading ended shortly thereafter as the grandmother would convey nothing more of import. I could have asked other spirits or Running Water for more information, but futurizing only really works when a particular spirit really wants to convey something. This girl had blown her chance.

To get a glimpse of the future you have to communicate with the past, because the only person who can tell you with any authority what will happen in your future is among those in the spirit world. The acid test in deciding whether a medium is any good or not is surely what they are able to tell you about your life to date. Unless the medium can give specific details of what has happened before – names, dates, things that make you sit up and say yes, that is really so and so, or that did happen – then you should not place any faith in what the medium has to say about future events. The test of any mediumship or futurizing is that it must be evidential.

*

A spirit guide may not tell you anything to interfere with your fate line, but this does not mean that they won't warn you about a tragic event such as an avoidable accident or an untimely death. There are some things that happen to people that are just not supposed to. Violent murders, accidents, suicides are the kind of events that sometimes defy what might have been ordained for us. If a spirit tells me during a reading about something like this then it is usually because it can be prevented. On the other hand, should no warning be made, then it is because this is our fate.

If a person comes for a reading wanting to know when and where they will pass over, it is unlikely that they will get an answer. I will not be given a message to pass on to the young man sitting in my reading room that he will pass away in his sleep at the grand old age of ninety-seven. We are only told of deaths or accidents if they are not supposed to happen. A spirit guide may warn a person through me not to travel by boat in the near future because they can see that there will be a drowning, which is not their destined death. Of course, it is up to the individual to decide whether he or she should heed this advice; it becomes the path that they choose to take. I can't prevent the accident from happening, should they decide to take that path; I am only a messenger, not God. Once they leave my reading room it is up to them.

Last year I read for a woman who had a teenage son. I told her during the reading that I was very concerned about the lad. I said I felt that he had fallen in with a young chap who was a bit wild. I named the friend. The woman told me that her son did indeed have a new friend with that name, but that he did not match that description and that her son was a model young man. She was adamant about it. But her spirit guides just kept going on and on about this lad and his friend. They told me that they went out every Sunday together and that they rode a red motorcycle. The woman confirmed that the two boys spent most Sundays in each other's company, but she had no knowledge of a bike. Her son, she said, knew the dangers of motorcycles and would never ride one, and in any case he didn't have a licence. But this image wouldn't leave me, and then I had this terrible sense of foreboding. I kept hearing the word 'accident' in my head and tried to warn her. There was nothing else in this reading. It was just about her son and her bike. By the end of it I think I had managed to instill some sense that something bad was about to happen, but I don't think that at the time she was wholly convinced by my reading. She told me at her next reading that she had questioned her son about the bike on her return, and he had denied it. Nevertheless, on the following Sunday when her son's friend came to call, she wouldn't let her boy out of the house. They had a row, and she ended up locking him in the bathroom. Later on that day she received a call from the friend. There had been an accident involving one of her son's classmates. The boy, who had been riding a red motorcycle, had been killed instantly.

Futurizing is hard work. Not because it is difficult communicating with the spirits themselves but because sometimes the messages that you are asked to relay seem so ridiculous, so improbable and hard to believe. There have been times when I have relayed a message to a person about their future and they have just looked at me blankly, but nine out of ten times they will later write to let me know that what was predicted has actually happened.

Some years ago a woman came to see me for a reading. I am not very good with faces, and when you read twenty people a week it is difficult to remember everyone. But there was something very familiar about this woman. I kept thinking to myself, 'You know her.' I asked her if I had read for her before. She said yes, and told me that she had come to see me ten years ago.

'In fact,' she said, 'I have come to apologize to you, Rita. When I last came to see you I had just come through a terrible divorce. I hated that man with all my heart, and vowed that I would never speak to him again. You told me that I had just divorced but that I would remarry the man. I couldn't believe you had the audacity to predict such a preposterous thing, and I just laughed out loud at you.'

The woman told me that her husband had run off with his teenage secretary, taking all his wife's savings, to the tune of £215,000, with him. I had told her that however much she hated him at that moment she would forgive him one day. I said that they would meet again, in an unusual situation, that they would fall in love all over again, and that he would repay her all the money he had stolen from her, to the exact figure. They would remarry, but he would only live two years after that.

Sure enough, they did meet again. They bumped into each other abroad and fell in love once more. They remarried and he passed away two years later, on their second wedding anniversary.

'The only thing that you seemed to have got wrong,' the woman said, 'was the money. He never gave me a penny while he was alive, but I didn't mind because I was happy again. Then after he died I received a letter from an insurance firm. He had taken out a policy before we had met again for the full amount of what he owed me – £215,000.

*

There is another aspect of futurizing which can prove to be problematic. It is when a person takes a prediction too far. A person I read for should not give up on life and wait for a prediction to happen. Just because it has been predicted that a young woman will meet the man she is destined to marry on a mountain, for example, does not mean she should necessarily give up her social life and enrol herself on a hill-walking course. Futurizing can be helpful, but we should not let it rule our lives. You should not try to consciously live out predictions either.

A young lady visited me last summer who seemed concerned that she had not met anyone in her life with whom she could have a serious relationship. During her reading her spirit guide told me that she should not worry as she would one day meet a wonderful person and have a long lasting relationship with him. She would meet him while she was on holiday, and that the first thing that he would ask her was if she would like a drink. It turned out that the girl in question was booked to go on holiday with some friends in Spain later that month. She later told me that on the first night she was offered a cocktail by a man staying in the same hotel. This was no surprise, since the girl was really very attractive. She accepted and, although as she later admitted to me she didn't like him that much, he was foreign so communication was difficult and they had little in common, they began having a relationship.

But when she returned to England he did not contact her again. She came to see me soon afterwards and was very unhappy. I told her to cheer up as I felt that she was about to win something. Weeks later she received a letter informing her that she had won a competition, the prize being a holiday in France. She was sitting on her own at the bar on the ferry when the barman asked her if he could buy her drink. She said afterwards she thought nothing of the reading at the time, and that he was just being friendly because she was sitting there looking so miserable. They married some months ago.

Nine

MY LIFE AS A MEDIUM

PEOPLE OFTEN tell me how lucky I am to possess the skills I have. They tell me how they would like to be able to communicate with the spirit world, to know what the future holds for them. Mediumship certainly is very rewarding. You only have to see a person's face after you have made contact with their spirits to see that and there is little in life that gives me greater pleasure than to help people realize that there is life after death. When I read for a mother who has lost her child in an accident, and I am able through spiritual communication to assure her that her child lives on, then I know, even if I once had my doubts, that what I am doing is right. Mediumship is indeed a 'gift'.

But for all its rewards, there are still moments when I wish that I was living an ordinary life. Reading for people can be very draining and difficult to cope with. I have seen so much suffering over the years, so much grief, and it's hard to walk away from something like that at the end of the day and carry on with your own life. What's more, mediumship is not something you can turn on and off when it suits you. The gift is with you twenty-four hours a day. To an extent you can learn to control it by creating moments when you are specifically more in tune to spirit, by allowing yourself time to be quiet and focused, to empty your head of other thoughts and distractions and make yourself more open to the spirit messages. But even if at times you allow yourself to be more available to the spirits than at others, sensory perceptions, clairaudience, and clairvoyance are not things that can be fully 'turned off'.

I also firmly believe that mediumship is not an occupation but a vocation. If I receive a telephone call in the evening from someone who feels that they just cannot cope with life any more, I know that I will have to do my best there and then to try and help them, even if I'm technically 'off duty'. But it is not just the people who I read for that call upon me for help. Spirits also come to me throughout the day and the night.

Recently I was woken at two o'clock in the morning by the spirit of a young girl called Stephanie. I had read for her mother, who lived in Florida, some months before. Stephanie was asking me to contact her mother, saying it was urgent and that I must tell her 'Dad will be OK.' I had no idea what this meant, and have to admit that I felt somewhat foolish making the telephone call to these relative strangers in America. But when I did eventually get through to Stephanie's mother, she knew exactly what the message meant. She told me that she had just come in from the hospital because her husband, Stephanie's father, had suffered a stroke. And she called me back later to say that the doctors had indeed said that he would be 'OK', even though they had all at first had their doubts.

Daily life as a medium can be quite strange. The simplest everyday task, which most people take for granted, such as a trip to the shops, can be literally interrupted by spiritual intervention. But you have to be realistic about what you can actually achieve. I was once standing at the supermarket checkout when a voice in my head said, 'Tell that young girl there that Mam is here, and that I want a word.' The girl was packing my bags and I was panicking, thinking, 'What on earth shall I do? What if that young woman doesn't want to know? What if she doesn't believe in spirit and thinks I'm mad?' I was also aware that there was a long queue behind me, and I didn't think that the other customers would be too pleased if I launched into a reading over my shopping basket. I smiled at her and left it at that, hoping that at some stage we would have another chance to speak. But there have been other occasions when I have felt a compulsion to pass a message on, whatever the circumstances. For example, I was once sitting in a pub in Lincolnshire having a quiet drink with Mo, when I noticed a man and a woman sitting at the table next to ours. They weren't saying much and I was struck by how pensive and sad she looked. Then I started hearing a man's voice in my head. He wanted to talk to her, and he wouldn't leave me alone. Again, I didn't know what to do. I didn't want to intrude in this woman's life, but the voice wouldn't go away. I had the feeling that something terrible had happened to this spirit and that he had been very close to the woman. She soon finished the last of her drink, and was picking her bag up to leave. I made Mo go after her. 'I'm sorry to bother you', he said when he caught up with her, 'but Rita would like a word.' Heaven knows what she thought, but she came over to the table anyway.

'You had a brother, didn't you?' I said. She looked bewildered. 'I'm sorry, it's just that I'm a medium. I didn't want to bother you, but he won't go away. He's desperate to speak to you.'

She sat down. 'Yes, I did have a brother, but he died some months ago,' she said.

'Was he shot?' I asked.

The woman nodded. She told me that her brother had been murdered. I asked her if she would like to speak with him, she said yes. The reading went well and was extremely moving for us both. I was glad at the end of it that I had pursued her after all, and the woman told me that it had helped her a great deal.

Spirits don't just talk to mediums at odd times; they sometimes actually like to come and visit. Mo has seen little Lara in our house on several occasions. She likes to sit on the corner of my chair in the reading room and look out of the window. And once we were driving up the road when we passed a friend in his car, coming in the other direction. He waved to us. When I saw him again later on that day he said to me, 'So, you were out with your grandchildren today, were you?' I couldn't think what he was going on about: my two young granddaughters had been at school all day. 'What made you say that?' I asked him. 'I swear I saw them with you today. You had two children in the back of the car when I passed you.'

As I've explained, there are two types of medium, those who are clairvoyant and those who are clairaudient. Clairvoyance, which literally translates as clear vision, is the ability to *see* images and symbols which have been passed on to the medium from the spirit world. Clairaudience, or clear 'hearing', is the ability to *hear* spirit messages. Most mediums do have the ability both to hear and see spirit messages, but they tend to work with the sense which is the strongest. I often do receive clairvoyant images, but the majority of spiritual messages that I receive are clairaudient.

But when a medium hears or see spirits they are not actually utilizing their physical eyes or ears. It's like having an inner ear, or another sight beyond the material world. For my part, I feel the messages coming to me through my solar plexus, which turns into the sensation of having a voice within my head. It's quite distinct from anything you would normally hear in your ear.

Being clairaudient means that I am able to give readings over the telephone. The contact that I am making with the spirit world and the messages which I am receiving are actually audible to me. It is like having a three-way conversation, or a conference call. I do not even have to see the person for whom I am reading for the mediumship to work; the channel between the recipient and the spirits is still as strong and my role in the reading is similar to that of a radio transmitter. A telephone reading is just as effective as if somebody came to me in person.

The reception of a message can also vary. Sometimes the message will come through very clearly, in others it might be quite faint and difficult to make out. As I've said before, when a spirit is trying to tell me his or her name I might only be able to make out the first initial to begin with, the name usually following on quite quickly after that. When I was reading for Ryan's parents, for example, I was not sure if I was hearing Brian or Ryan to start off with. This was because his voice was quite faint, and it may have also had something to do with the fact that I was also getting his strong South African accent which I wasn't used to. Letters that are phoentically similar, such as 'J' and a soft 'G', are always quite difficult to distinguish, but I find that over the course of a reading I should be able to make sense of what I am hearing!

When a person comes for a reading, especially if it is the first time that they have visited a medium, I like to chat with them beforehand. I do this to put them at their ease. Contacting spirit can be quite a harrowing experience, and I find that most people whom I read for the first time are a little nervous about the process. I also helps me to get an idea of what the person I am reading for is like, so that I know how to broach certain subjects. You see, I don't like to keep things from people who come for a reading, but I need to find out how best to pass the message on. If a spirit tells me something it's because they want something to be known. If a person has been shocked by the passing of a loved one, I will take the reading very slowly, and will tread more gently than I might do otherwise. If I am giving a telephone reading, then I will begin by asking that person what their star sign is, to give me a rough idea of their personality and how they will take things. Fire signs, on the whole, can take on board almost anything you say. Water signs tend to be more sensitive, so I keep the conversation in neutral areas. I am not trying to find out any clues about the person to help me to guess at things, I just want us both to feel comfortable before we begin.

But once the reading has begun I prefer it if the recipient doesn't talk at all. This way the medium avoids autosuggestion, or the reading being influenced by the recipient's responses. I am, after all, only human and if somebody starts talking to me about their life, it is bound to have some influence on what I say to them in their reading. I had a terrible time once with a lady who just would not stop talking to me and telling me all about her life before I even had a chance. By the end of it I wondered why she had bothered coming to me, as it was clear she wasn't interested in anything her spirits had to say!

The only thing that I will ask a person is whether they have known anyone in the past five years who has passed over. The question is essentially rhetorical. I do not expect an answer, nor do I really want to know from them. I ask this in order that the person will concentrate their minds on these people, thus encouraging the spirits to come forward. There may well be more than one, and on some occasions they will all start talking at once, which can be quite confusing.

The spirit will give me some piece of information by which they hope you will be able to identify them. It could be their name, their relationship to you, the way in which they died. Sometimes they are less straightforward, for example, naming a pub where you both used to drink, the name of your dog, or using your nickname. Often these messages seem puzzling to me, but will make perfect sense to the recipient. You see, spirits want us to know and believe that it is really them speaking. These small, often obscure details enable the person being read for to recognize them and know that it really is them there. Lara, for example, told me the name of one of her brother's cuddly toys when her mother Beverly came to see me.

Spirits are not sinister, nor are they out to scare you. When they come through they are essentially as they were in this life, and usually like to share a joke and have a laugh. Whilst my own voice does not change when passing on messages, I am told I tend to adopt the characteristics of speech that the spirit had in this life. In a good reading the messages that I pass on will be characteristic, even idiosyncratic, and succeed almost immediately in establishing the identity of the transmitter.

Having read for so many people, it is difficult for me to

describe the impact that such messages can have. Connie, the mother of Rebecca, whom I have mentioned before and who lives in America, offered to describe what a reading is like in her own words.

Becky was an extremely funny and cheeky young girl. And it really comes through in her readings! One time she mentioned the underwear that I had on; another time she laughed at my new haircut, and said that she knew that I hated it. What I like about the messages I get from Becky is that they are so personal – they could only be from her for me. She told me once during a telephone reading with Rita that the circuit fuses in my electrical box had gone. She was right, of course, but on a nine-dollar-a-minute call from Las Vegas to Derbyshire, I'm thinking, 'Hey, I don't want to know about my electrics! What about the important things?' But in a way I suppose that these are the important things. They show that not only is Rita really talking to Rebecca, but that my daughter is with me in my life still.

To be able to hear messages from the spirit world clearly I must have the right environment to work in. For a medium, any distraction or noise can be extremely off-putting. I find I have to work in a quiet place where I feel comfortable and am able to concentrate wholly on what I am doing. When we first moved to Ash House, my first priority was to establish such an environment, somewhere friendly and light. I chose a warm, sunny room at the front of the house, which I call my reading room. There are no Ouija boards, no pyramids or props. I don't even use a crystal ball. There's an armchair by the window, which I sit in, and a sofa for the people who come and see me. There is also a crucifix on the cabinet, and a copy of the Bible by my armchair, because I believe in God, and that he should be part of my work. I believe he also protects me. On the walls hang hundreds of photographs of people I have got in spirit. Most of them are of young children, who I call my spirit children. I like to have them round me when I read.

I created this room not only for me and my clients but also for the spirits. Contrary to what you may have seen in films, spirits don't like dark, gloomy rooms and houses. They like a place that is safe and where they know they are welcome. When I had the reading room wallpapered recently, the decorators found it very difficult to work in there. They said they felt as though they were working in slow motion. I think that my spirit children didn't like the fact that their pictures had been taken down in order to prepare the walls for the job. Despite the decorators' lethargy, I've never seen a team of workmen so keen to finish a job in my life!

Objectivity is an important part of my work. You may not necessarily like the person who is sitting in front of you, or approve of what they have done in their lives, but it is not your role as a medium to judge them. I am here to help people, and I have to remain impartial; personal feelings must not come out, people live their lives in their own ways. I might pick up on something that an individual has done that I might not approve of, but I cannot hold that against them. Remember, I am only passing on messages from spirit, whether about the past or future. I can advise people if they ask me to, but I do that in a separate capacity.

It is important to establish trust right at the start. I view my work as being like that of a doctor or a priest, in that I would never discuss the readings of someone if they asked me not to. What happens within the walls of my reading room should not go any further than that. I have not named and discussed people in this book without their permission.

There are occasions when I will decide not to read a person. This only happens when I think that they might be a danger to me, or to my family, or themselves. Usually, if a person has committed some serious crime then I certainly prefer not to read them. I had a very disturbing experience once with a man who came to contact the spirit of his dead daughter. I thought nothing of it when the reading began but I soon started to get a bad feeling about him. His daughter came through and I saw her first before I heard her, which was unusual in itself. I remember it vividly; she was wearing a bright red dress. Then she started to talk to me.

I looked up at the man. 'My God, you murdered her, didn't you?' I asked, looking him straight in the eye. The girl was telling me that her boyfriend had been prosecuted for the crime instead.

'God forgive me,' he said, but with little sincerity.

'I doubt he will,' I replied. 'Please leave. I cannot read a man who has no remorse.'

Another situation where I will avoid reading for people is if I feel that they have become too dependent on me. As much as it pains me to do so, if I feel that someone has become 'hooked' on readings I will try and suggest that we not meet for some time, maybe a year or so. Losing someone is very hard, and I understand that a good reading can be a helpful and cathartic experience. But I cannot live the life of someone who has gone, and people should not try to live that life through me either. Whilst I do not believe in death as such, I do believe that people have passed over into another world and we must let them live that new life.

There are also times when I will not be able to get anyone in spirit. This may be because I am simply not up to it – I am feeling physically drained, or emotionally preoccupied. In such situations I will give the person their money back. If I cannot get anyone in spirit there is no reading; it's as simple as that. You can't make these kinds of things up and it would be irresponsible to do so. You are dealing with other people's lives! Sometimes, however, the fault may not be mine alone – sometimes a spirit may just refuse to come. I read for a lady for whom the only message I was getting was extremely strange. 'I'm sorry to ask you this,' I said to the lady, 'but do you know anyone who has "rot to death"?' I had never heard of anyone 'rotting to death' before, but the woman obviously did. She clasped her hand to her mouth. 'My mother!' she said. 'Oh God, I'm so sorry,' she kept saying.

The woman had been very young when her elderly mother got ill. She had been bedridden for some time, and her daughter had not known how to take care of her properly. She went out one weekend, leaving her mother on her own. There was heavy snow, and the woman was unable to get back that night. In fact, she didn't return for some days. When she did, she found her mother had died, that she had literally died from rot, having no one to care for her. I did feel very sorry for this woman, as she obviously felt very guilty, but it was no use. The spirit of her mother did not want to talk to her, and the reading ended.

I don't like to work in front of large crowds or audiences. I prefer to read on a one-to-one basis, or in front of a group who know each other well. Readings are very personal experiences. I am not here to perform for people, but to help them. It is not enough for me to just 'get' someone in spirit, when there is the opportunity to *speak* to the spirit world we should use it properly. I don't like stage psychic shows or platform readings, not because I don't approve of them, but because I am always concerned that a spirit might want to say something of an intimate nature to the recipient, something that the person might not want a group of strangers to know about.

Spirits aren't there just to back a medium up, coming along to say 'hello'. If they have the chance of making contact with you, then they'll want to talk to you properly. They might want to tell you how they came to pass over, what happened to them, what you are worried about. The purpose of my work is to help people, not to entertain others.

Some years ago I received an invitation from a group of women holding a charity evening in Surrey. They asked me whether I would like to attend a dinner and afterwards talk about my work. I accepted. On the appointed evening I arrived at the address, having travelled south from Derbyshire, and rang the bell. I was ushered in, but rather than being shown the dining room where all the guests were already seated, I was ushered instead into a small ante-room. 'Can you wait in here, Mrs Rogers? We'll be with you after we've finished dinner, and then the fun will begin,' said the hostess, handing me a bottle of gin.

It did not take me long to realize what was going on. I had been invited to this house to provide the after-dinner entertainment! I was here not to talk about my work, but to give readings to a group of 'ladies who lunch'. I take my work seriously, and to have it described as a bit of 'fun', or to be seen as something of a cabaret act infuriated me. I did think about leaving there and then, but then I thought to myself, if that's what they want, that's what they'll get. We *could* have some 'fun' here. I nursed my gin (which I never usually drink), and waited.

After dinner, they all duly came together in the drawing room. The hostess beckoned to me to start. I summoned my spirit guides and asked them for help. Looking back I think that the spirits must have been as rattled as I was, for the messages they were giving me were so mischievous. As I looked around, I also swear I have never seen so many red faces in one room – they all had something to hide. I contacted the spirit of a woman sitting at the back. 'He's telling me about your termination,' I said. The poor woman turned white, and you should have seen the looks she got from the others. Then a spirit started on about another woman's lover, and then about another's extra-marital affairs. And so it went on! Normally, I would never have dared say anything like this to a crowd, which is why I avoid big meetings and I was as discreet as I felt I could be. Nevertheless, one by one the plums fell from the mouths of those ladies, and I have to admit I enjoyed every single minute of it.

Mediumship comes into being when innate psychic powers are developed in close co-operation with spirit guides. These are qualified because of their advanced evolutionary state in spirit to act as tutors in these matters. But mediumship is not the only means of achieving a level of psychic insight. There are many different ways of reading a person, be it their past, their present or their future, without having direct communication with the spirit world. You can read a person by simply looking at their aura – the transparent, luminous substance which we believe surrounds the body. Although the aura is not visible to the lay person's eyes, we do all have one. You can read a person simply by looking at the colour of their aura, and its width. The colours of the aura denote temperament, emotion and character. Yellow shows intellect and wisdom, red denotes anger, orange is drive and ambition, blue implies devotion and love, while green is jealousy and grey, fear. A well-adjusted, happy, healthy person's aura will be bright and bluey-green in colour, and will be wide in breadth. A person who is emotionally or physically weak will have a much fainter aura; a person who has not long in this world will have a very thin aura. People who are spiritual tend to have golden auras, like my grandmother had, and the medium who visited me at Doe Lea.

Another way of reading someone is through the ancient art of palmistry. Your palm is an intrinsic part of you and the way its lines have formed reflects your destiny; it tells you your lifespan, how many marriages and children you have had or will have. It is what I call your life map. It tells you where you are going, but it does not tell you how you will get there, nor can it give any specifics. For this reason, palm reading is more open to autosuggestion, and the client prompts the reader.

The crystal ball tells you the journey you will make in life. Within the crystal ball I see small stars of light. When a person is given the ball and it is placed in their hand, the reader looks at the way the light interacts with these tiny stars. It is a tool, but again does not offer specifics.

Although I can read palms and I own a Romany crystal ball, I tend not to use them in my work as I find them less reliable and less informative than actually talking to spirits. It is also possible to take a person's belonging and feel something from that. This is called psychometry, and it is often practised with a piece of jewellery. It works because that jewellery, like your palm and your aura, belongs to you. But it's use is also limited as it can only tell you about the owner of the article themselves, and of the person who gave it to them.

Then there is the Tarot. The Tarot is a set of traditional fortune-telling cards which dates back to the fourteenth century. There are seventy-eight cards in all, which are divided into two sets. The Minor Arcana has fifty-six cards, the Major Arcana twenty-two. Each card is printed with an allegorical figure which holds a special meaning. The idea is that when the cards are shuffled by the person wanting to know their future, and then laid down by the reader of the cards, a map of one's past, present and future can be read by interpreting the pattern of these symbols. Personally I do not like this method of reading. My problem with it is purely common-sensical, that it is reliant on the interpretation of the reader. Should you have your cards read more than once, the odds that they will be laid out in the same sequence each time are slim. But you do not have two lives! How you can read anyone accurately from a deck of cards baffles me. The cards can't belong to you. But your spirits, palm, jewellery and aura do.

I am also very against the use of the Ouija board. Traditionally, a Ouija board is circular in shape and is marked with the letters of the alphabet and the words 'yes', 'no', and 'goodbye'. The board has a pointer, called a planchette, which is designed in such a way that it glides over the letters, then stops of its own volition. The letters it points to may be read as messages, which are believed to come from the spirit world. But I would not advise anyone interested in spiritualism and psychic power to have anything to do with the board or its messages. The spirits contacted through the Ouija board are from the first world, or are earthbound spirits. They have not come to help you or give you love and guidance, but to create trouble. The spirits that you would wish to contact will not come through to you in this way; they will only come through where there is love, and it is safe. Even though I am a medium, I personally would be very wary of having any contact with these spirits. I don't believe any good can come out of this practice, and people should be warned that it is very dangerous to meddle with the unknown.

*

I tend not to have much contact with other mediums today. I work with my gift on my own, and do not belong to any institution or psychic society. However, I did have the greatest respect for Doris Stokes. Although I never met her while she was alive, I like to think we have met in another dimension, and that there is a spiritual link between us now. In the summer of 1990 I was visited by a couple who had travelled from down south. As with all such readings I had never met this couple before, and I didn't know anything about them before they came to see me.

Having spent so many years practising as a medium, their visit shouldn't have caused me any concern. By now I was reading up to twenty people a week. But as soon as this couple set foot in my house, I began to feel nervous and suspicious. It was as though Running Water was trying to warn me about something. It wasn't the people them-selves who scared me, for they were extremely nice. It was more to do with why they had come.

My instincts were right. It transpired that the couple had been sent by a national tabloid newspaper who wanted to 'test' out my gift to see if I was 'genuine' or not. I didn't want to be tested like this – for I always say that I'm not in this business to prove myself – but I kept thinking that if I refused to co-operate they would say that I was a fraud, that I was making it all up, and those who don't believe in me would have won. Nor did I want to let my other clients down; I decided to rise to the challenge.

But as if all this wasn't bad enough the couple went on to tell me that the last medium they had visited was Doris Stokes. In fact, they had been two of the last people to be read by her before she passed away.

Doris Stokes was absolutely the queen of mediums. I believe that she was the greatest we have known this century, and there has never been any doubt that Doris was anything but the genuine article. Her messages were incredibly accurate, and the premonitions and predictions she gave were enough to convince even the most ardent of disbelievers that she really was conversing with spirits. Needless to say, she was a great showperson as well. Such was her confidence and skill that she was able to read in auditoriums filled with hundreds of people. But the thing that really set Doris apart from other mediums was her ability to truly connect with people. She realized that it was very important to relate to those she read to, that it was not just the spirit world she was talking to but ordinary folk.

Doris always liked to make people feel relaxed in her company, and what comes across in the transcripts and tapes of her readings is how much she enjoyed talking to a spirit, often sharing a joke with them. She may have gained notoriety, but she did not give up on her mission. Her message was simple enough: 'I'm here to pass on information from spirits to relatives and friends to prove that they live on in another dimension.'

So it was perhaps understandable that I was so apprehensive about this reading. I had been worried that I might not be able to connect with their spirits, and that as a result I would fail not only in the eyes of the press and the public, but more importantly with this couple. Now before the reading began, rather than summoning Running Water for his help, I turned to Doris for guidance. 'Doris,' I thought to myself, 'you, of all people, understand what this is like. Help me to pass on the messages, tell me about these people.'

My mind had been blank at that point, but then I heard her talking softly in my head. She was giving me impressions, places and signs. I could see light and dark, the initial 'Z', a vehicle of some sort, which became a boat, and I could see a lot of red and people in uniform – crewmen. I could feel that there had been an accident, that it had affected the lives of these people sitting in front of me. I could hear people screaming, and was struck by a strange crushing feeling.

Then a young man came to me in spirit. He was telling me that he had passed over in a ferry accident. He said his name, and that he was there with his girlfriend, who had also passed over in the accident. I got her name, that she was his fiancée, and that her sister was also there. He told me more about how he had died, that he had been trying to save others. He told me that his fiancée was not wearing her engagement ring when she died because it was still at the jewellers. He described the presents he had bought his family on the ferry: perfume for his mother, a bottle of aftershave for his father, and a Disney toy for his nephew.

After the reading ended, the couple told me that their son, aged nineteen, had died in the Zeebrugge ferry tragedy, when the *Herald of Free Enterprise* sank off the Belgian coast in March 1987. It was known from eyewitness reports that he had lost his life helping others to escape from the sinking ship. He had been travelling with his fiancée, aged twenty. She had indeed left her ring at the jewellers, and had been with her sister when she died. This family had been through a terrible ordeal, and were still coming to terms with their loss.

Had it not been for Doris's guidance, I doubt very much that I would have even been able to speak, let alone read for this couple. At the end of the reading they thanked me. Then they added that I had told them exactly what Doris had also said to them, and that our styles were very similar. 'You have carried on where Doris left off,' they said. It was the greatest compliment anyone could ever have paid me. I have always said that if I was considered half as good as Doris Stokes then I would be extremely happy.

Soon after, I opened a Sunday paper to find a whole story about me splashed across it. It did indeed recount the couple's visit to me. But in no way did it let on that they had tried to catch me out: the story was glowing.

Ten

THE MEDIUM AS DETECTIVE

THE COMMUNICATION that I have with the spirit world, and the messages that the spirits give me, sometimes enable me and the recipients of these messages to make sense of the many unanswered questions that surround a person's death.

Spirits like to begin readings by talking about how they passed away. Often this can be a very harrowing experience for the person for whom I am reading, and I will need to make a decision as to whether what they are saying is going to be helpful or not to that person. Sometimes you have to spare the family the most distressing details, focusing instead on the fact that the person is safe, secure and, most importantly, now without pain. Such messages can be very helpful to relatives, particularly in the case of suicides or murders. But there are other ways as well in which spirits can help solve mysteries: for example, like the time when I was able to find the lost share certificates for the woman in Skegness; or when I am able to help an elderly woman find a piece of jewellery that has been missing for some years. These situations can be very rewarding. Although I don't like to set myself up as some kind of spiritual detective, more often than not I will find myself helping to piece together some mystery as a result of a reading. Whether it is discovering something about a death or finding a missing person, the spirits will always give the answers.

In the winter of 1984 I received a telephone call from an army General who was based in Inverness. To my astonishment he said that he needed my help. Two of his soldiers had gone missing in the Cairngorms and he was wondering whether I might be able to locate them. I was hesitant about committing myself to such a task, since for someone to come through in spirit there must be some kind of connection between the recipient and the spirit, and I did not know the General. I was about to end the conversation when he told me that in 1976 I had given a reading at a psychic fair I had gone to when I was just starting out to one of the missing men, a Sergeant called Paul Rodgers, then a Corporal. The General told me that Sergeant Rodgers had raved about the reading I had given him, and he had been amazed that so many of the predictions I had given him had afterwards come about. I had predicted his promotion and that sort of thing, but perhaps more ominously I had told him that one day he

would be lost in the mountains. The General asked me if
I would help to ease the uncertainty surrounding the case,
and at the very least tell the missing man's wife whether
he was alive or not.

Half an hour later I found myself giving a reading to
the Sergeant's father. A voice came through loud and
clear, which told me that his wife was Linda, and the
name of the other missing man. And then he began telling
me very precisely where they were. I told the General,
and, a search began at once. But I also knew then that
Sergeant Rodgers had not yet passed away. To have heard
his voice would have meant that he was already in spirit,
but what I was hearing was the voice of his colleague, who
had passed over. He was beyond help, but what he wanted
me to do now was to save the life of his friend.

A helicopter circled the area that had been described
to me. I was in constant contact with the pilot, giving him
directions and landmarks. I think then that the pilot
thought that I was a witch or something. He seemed to be
laughing at me, and I knew that he didn't really believe in
what I was doing or saying to him. Because of the heavy
snow the chopper could find no trace of the soldiers, and
because of the hazardous weather conditions they were
forced to abandon their search. But the next day they
located the missing men, buried in snow in the same area
I had described to the pilot the previous day. It was too

late; both men had died from exposure. Had the weather not been so bad the day before, Paul Rodgers might have been saved, but it was not to be. The pilot admitted to me later that he felt he had to take back everything he had said.

Initially, I was frustrated. You see, I knew that the man who had contacted me had been not quite at the top of a mountain, and he was indeed found buried in snow in such a spot. He had told me Paul Rodgers was further up, and that he had injured his ankle so he was unable to walk. I could see that he had built himself something of an igloo to keep warm in the snowstorm, but the blizzard was so heavy it had quickly covered him up and trapped him. This is why the helicopter wasn't able to spot him, even though I knew he could hear it whirring. They found the shelter when they recovered the body. I also sensed that it was at midnight that he passed over, and this accorded with the doctor's report when the bodies were examined. We had been so close. But the main thing was that we had, through the help of Sergeant Rodgers's friend, tried our best.

When Helen came for her first reading her daughters Laura and Emma immediately told me that they had lost their lives in a fire which had been started deliberately. 'They're telling me "Andrew" did it,' I said to Helen. Helen confirmed that this was true, the Andrew in question had just been prosecuted and is now serving a life sentence for what he did to her family.

Sometimes the details surrounding a passing can be harrowing and difficult for the recipient to have to listen to. In most cases we are well aware of that information anyway, so a spirit will not dwell on it too much. But there are times in my readings when a spirit will come through and talk of little else. In these cases it is because the circumstances of their deaths are not quite as they seem.

On 30 December 1990 Paul Jenkinson, a Lincolnshire teenager, fell from the top of a 100ft multi-storey car park in Lincoln city centre. He passed away two days later, on New Year's Day, from the injuries sustained during the fall. The inquest reported an open verdict, and the police said that there was no evidence to suggest that anyone else was there. The general feeling was that Paul had taken his own life, although the coroner found no proof that Paul had actually jumped.

Paul's mother, Sue, was not satisfied, 'Paul wasn't that sort of boy', she told me after our first reading. 'Something just isn't ringing true.' Unable to get the answers she needed through the conventional channels, Sue decided to visit me with her brother Brian some months later. Although I had been recommended through mutual acquaintances, I didn't know anything about her or her son when they arrived. But as soon as the reading began, Paul came through and was telling me over and over again that he didn't kill himself. This information confirmed what Sue had been thinking all along. She didn't believe that her son had jumped, or even that he was alone just before he fell.

This is her story.

I visited Rita Rogers three months after Paul's passing because I was so frustrated with the verdict I had been given by the court. I knew that Paul had been in some kind of trouble before he died, but I didn't believe he would take his own life. Perhaps it is a mother's instinct. I had known Paul for seventeen years. I knew what he was capable of. We went to Rita because she had a good reputation and because I wanted to go to someone who wasn't local, someone who would not have heard about the case. I had been to some mediums before but they just asked me lots of questions and told me nothing, not even a name. Rita got Paul's straight away. She was able to tell me things about Paul that convinced me that he was really talking to her, little, but very precise things – about his guitar, for example. He kept saying over and over that he didn't kill himself. She spoke of a tall building. That she was feeling a sensation similar to falling. She kept saying he was not alone.

Rita told me that before he died in hospital he had a black eye. He did. Rita said that he got in a scuffle, during which he had fallen over the edge; that a group of lads he had been avoiding for some time took him up to the top of the car park in order to get him to steal a car. Rita said that Paul had been extremely frightened and that there was a lad there who was part of a gang that hung out in the Monks Road area of the city, which was known to be quite rough. He had been bullying Paul. This gang was involved with drugs. She talked of Paul being edgy, and how he felt he had to watch his back. And Paul was forever locking doors behind him when he came in at night.

Before he died Paul truly seemed to be living in fear. He had stopped going down Monks Road, and would not open up. The night he died he had gone out to buy some cigarettes. He had taken some change and put it in his pocket, and to avoid the Monks Road he walked along the allotments instead. But he never did buy the fags. Rita knew exactly how much money he had in his pocket at the time when he was taken to hospital.

She said that she would stake her career on the fact that there had been more people there and that Paul had not set out to take his own life. I had hoped she might be able to give me names of the others involved, but she said that Paul was not ready to do that yet. She explained to me that spirits are not *vengeful, and that Paul would not want me to go after people but be happy with the knowledge that he was still around and that he was no longer living in fear.*

Rita also described Paul to me. It was as though she had a photo of him. She knew his long curly hair, the shape of his face. She told me he was seventeen, that he loved heavy metal music and that he had a guitar, which she described. I cannot begin to tell you how I felt. Somehow, even though I was not able to get the information that I had initially wanted, it didn't matter. I had better news. Paul was now OK, he was no longer frightened, and he was with me at all times.

Sue Jenkinson's story shows how spirits wish to clarify the circumstances of how they passed over, especially if a mistake has been made. Paul did not want his mother to seek revenge on those responsible because he knew that they would get their dues in the spirit world. What he wanted his mother to know by talking to her about his passing was that there was nothing she could have done to prevent it. It was inevitable, he knew it would happen sooner or later, but he did not want his mother to feel that she should have foreseen it, or feel that she was responsible for it. Paul wanted to end Sue's suffering and anxiety by letting her know the truth.

A couple of years ago I read for another woman called Sue, whose twenty-three-year-old son had actually taken his own life. Sue knew this, and she had seen it coming, but there were still many questions that needed to be answered before she could put the matter to rest once and for all. This is her story.

SUE

My granddaughter, Hayley, was murdered five years ago. A year later my son, Christopher, killed himself. I suppose he couldn't take the loss really. He had been extremely depressed, and felt that he could no longer go on living without her. He had been having problems before that, but he could never come to terms with his daughter's passing. He didn't have much in his life, but he adored that child. We all did.

Hayley was only one when she passed over. When the police found her she was covered in bruises from head to toe. CID called my house one afternoon and told us to come down to the hospital. It was a horrific experience, and I can't bring myself to describe it. How anyone could do such a thing to a baby I will never understand. She passed away in Christopher's arms.

Hayley had not been living with us at the time. In fact, we had not been allowed to see her since her mother had left Christopher and moved in with another man. The doctors said the blows she had endured had caused severe brain damage, but she died from her other injuries as well. The police would later confirm what we had always feared, that it was the new boyfriend who had done this to our Hayley. And that her mother had just let it happen. He is now in prison; she is with another man.

Christopher was in pieces. I knew then that he would never recover, but each day for a year we battled on, trying to survive. I was not surprised when I was told that Christopher had ended his life.

In many ways it was a release. It's difficult to explain, but how can you live after that? Christopher couldn't. If it hadn't been for him, I might have felt the same way too. After his passing I was finally able to grieve, for them both, something that I hadn't been able to do after Hayley's death because I had to be there as a mother for him. I wanted to be strong and go through the grieving process naturally. But then I met Rita, truly quite by chance, and things changed. I was wary of having a reading, but there were things that I desperately wanted to know, things that kept me up throughout the night. And there was something about Rita that made me trust her. I hadn't believed in this kind of thing before, although I did pray a lot, but not to anyone specific.

After the reading, I understood why my son had done this. I realized that there were many things that had been affecting him, all the pressures around him – I realized he had been suffering for years, and Hayley's death was the final straw. It was Rita who told me what was going on in Christopher's life. About his relationship with Hayley's mother and why and how that had ended. We had talked, but it was difficult for me to know how much we should discuss. And there were things that were going on that Christopher didn't want me to know about. It was as if he was in a great deal of danger. It turned out that he was being blackmailed and threatened, being told that they would take it out on his family if Christopher didn't come up with what they wanted. I can't go into the details because the investigation is still going on. But Rita said things to me that correlated with what the police said afterwards. Details about a car, a man whom she named, and so on.

People say that suicide is a selfish act. Now I disagree. I realize that what he did wasn't selfish but completely selfless. He took his life to protect all of us and because he was no longer for this world. It isn't a coward's way out and it took a great deal of courage.

Good came out of it too, in the end, and funny things too. I passed my driving test not long ago. It was my first time, so naturally I was quite proud. When I went to see Rita again she mentioned it straight away. She also knew that I had a car. I actually didn't like it, and had wanted to sell it for some time. Christopher told Rita that I would sell it and not to worry. And do you know that when I got home that night, I had a phone call and I sold it like that! Christopher had said during the

reading that I wanted a new car. 'You want a car that's you,'
he said. I couldn't really think what he was on about. But the
next day I went off to buy a car and found what I was looking
for. When I got home I realized what he had meant. On the
number plate there was 'ST' – my initials, Susan Turner.

In cases where spirits have been murdered they will be
keen to get this message across as soon as a reading begins.
As I have said before, this is not because they are seeking
vengeance for their own deaths. It may be that they want
their family or friends to be aware of how they died and
who was to blame so as to set their minds at rest, or to
prevent such a terrible crime happening to someone else.

Some years ago I gave a reading to a young woman who
visited my house. As the reading began I got in spirit a
middle-aged woman. However, the young woman had no
recollection of anyone who had passed over of this age.
'Are you sure?' I asked. 'She's very keen to talk to you.
She's telling me she was murdered.' 'Oh, my God!' said
the young woman. 'That's my best friend's grandmother.'
The young woman contacted her friend and sure enough,
she booked an appointment for a reading, bringing a
policeman with her when she came. The spirit told me
that she had lived in a farmhouse in Norfolk; that one
evening she had taken a stroll, as she did every night, to
the woods. She noticed when she was there that there was

a car. She told me about the car, that it was an estate car, with a wire grill separating the boot area from the rest of the vehicle. In the boot was a dog; in the front seat a man. She said he came from behind her, while she was walking and, for no reason, stabbed her in the back, leaving her there to die. She described the wood where it happened, giving me a radius of twenty miles in which the crime had taken place. The spirit showed me a caravan site and said that was where the man lived. The policeman seemed agitated during the reading, and wrote down everything I said. Afterwards he told me that everything that I had described about the location and the way in which she had been killed fitted into what they had discovered so far. The description of the woodland was accurate, and a Volvo estate car had been traced as having been in the area that night. They had found a man some weeks later who owned an estate car with a grille at the back. He was the prime suspect in the murder inquiry. And they discovered that he lived alone with a dog on a caravan site.

Over the years I have been visited by the police, looking for help with their cases, on a number of occasions. I try as much as I can to assist them with their investigations, but it is often quite frustrating for both parties involved. Whilst I may be able to hear and see things that point them in the right direction, the police obviously need solid evidence before they can bring anyone to trial. Often the lead I will give them may result in them stumbling on the evidence that they need, but they do need to work with more than the testimony of a spirit under British law. As a medium I must have a *de facto* relationship with the police. Sometimes we will work on things directly together. More often the information that I get will come out of a regular reading, and it will be passed on to the police or detectives by the person I have read for. The police can then choose to do with it what they wish.

For example, a while ago I was visited by a woman and her sister. The woman was distraught as her thirteen-year-old daughter had gone missing. She had disappeared months before, and there was no sign of her. The child came through in spirit, so I knew that she had passed over. It was information that her mother, deep down, already knew. The child said she had been murdered, and she said that she had been buried under water. She told me who had done this to her. I am not sure whether the person was ever prosecuted, but a week after the reading the police dredged the canal near her home and found her body.

The messages that I am sent from the spirit world are not just about past events, or crimes which have already been committed. Often they are related to things which have yet to happen. These premonitions can be quite strong, and sometimes come in the form of a dream. Before the TWA disaster I dreamt that there would be a plane crash, a couple of nights before the tragedy took place. On other occasions I will hear a message, or see a flash of a picture in my mind. Sometimes I will just look at a car and get this feeling that there is something wrong with it. 'You've got a red van, haven't you?' I asked a friend recently. 'Get those brakes looked at.' I'm not sure why I said it, I know nothing about cars, and don't even have a driving licence. My friend was slightly bewildered as the van had only just passed its MOT, but knowing my reputation he did not feel it was wise to let my warning pass. He took the van to the garage that afternoon, only to find that the brake mechanism was worn down to its rivets. I also always get strong feelings about buildings, even from just crossing the threshold. I will suddenly get a feeling in my stomach, like having butterflies, and I will sense something about the place. It could be that there will be a fire, an explosion of some kind, a murder or just simply that the occupants will suffer unhappiness whilst under that roof.

Often my involvement in a case may be quite unintentional. I may just start hearing and sensing things even though I have no direct relationship with the people involved in a case. In the autumn of 1987 I had such an experience. I had gone for my annual break to the island of Jersey, a place I love. It was a holiday for me, and as such I had no desire whatsoever to start getting involved with readings. But it was not to be that way – the holiday turned out to be like a game of Cluedo.

A murder had taken place on the island. I was getting strange images in my head, of people, places, objects and murder weapons. But at the time I could not make any sense of them at all.

As the newspaper reports from the time recount, on the evening of 10 October 1987 Elizabeth and Nicholas Newell went out for dinner at the Sea Crest Hotel, Jersey, with their two sons Roderick and Mark, to celebrate Elizabeth's birthday. Elizabeth, forty-eight, and Nicholas, fifty-six, were both schoolteachers who lived on the island, in a bungalow at Clos de l'Atlantique, St Brelade. That dinner was the last time that the couple were seen alive. They were reported missing some days later. The following account of my involvement with the case has been given by Jean, a resident on the island and a friend of the Newell family. I had met Jean some years before on the island, and I had started reading for her.

The Newells had been good friends of mine. I would play tennis with Elizabeth quite often. The children had a very strict upbringing, but no one would have ever thought that things would end up like this.

Rita had come to the island for a break. She did not know much about the case at the time. She knew that people had gone missing, but we had not really discussed the details of it. It turned out that even before she had read any newspapers, she had said to a friend of ours before she left for Jersey that she had a feeling that something very bad had happened here, but she didn't know to whom. She said that she felt a man and wife had been murdered, and that this man had a twin brother.

When I met up with Rita in Jersey, we went for a walk. I remember that day very well. We were sitting on the rocks at Bouly Bay. The investigation as to the whereabouts of the Newells was underway. There had been reports in the papers of their disappearance, but Rita hadn't read them or seen any photographs of the couple. We were standing on the beach when she said that there were two people sitting on the cliff above us. We were quite alone on the beach, and I remember thinking it odd that there would be people up on the cliff, as it formed a pinnacle. Rita pointed up to them, but I could see nothing. There was no one there. Rita was adamant, and she described them to me. There was a man and a woman, in their mid-forties to -fifties. She said that the man was wearing heavy-rimmed spectacles, and that the woman had very red shoulder-length hair. They appeared to be pointing down to the ground. 'I think that they are trying to tell me that they have been buried,' she said. It sounded like Nicholas and Elizabeth, but I didn't say anything to her.

Later she told me that she was getting images she couldn't get out of her head. She could see a restaurant table and four people, they were toasting something, then a room with yellow and green decor. In a sitting room she could see a coffee table with three glasses on it. (This was later confirmed by a Sergeant I talked to who was investigating the case.) She could feel an immense heat and she said that she felt that two people had been murdered there. She felt that another murder had taken place in the bedroom, and she could see a lot of red, which she thought was blood. She then told me that she felt that there was also a red van involved. There had been no mention of this at the time in any of the newspapers.

Then she spoke of a bag, inside which was a selection of items that belonged to the couple. She said that it was hidden in woodlands on the island.

I informed the Sergeant working on the case. They combed a large area of woodland in the northern area of the island, where Rita had told me she'd seen something. There they found a bag containing a pair of glasses and the couple's belongings. She said as the weeks went on that she was convinced that this couple had been murdered by one of their sons, but that she could see the other son helping to dispose of the bodies. She described the bags that they used. Again, this was later confirmed by the evidence given in the trial. I was quite stunned *by what Rita was saying. Of course, none of us were to know exactly how accurate Rita's readings were until many years later when the boys were prosecuted, for only then did a lot of these details begin to emerge as physical and verbal evidence separately admitted in court.*

On 8 August 1994 Roderick and Mark Newell were sent to jail for the murder of their parents. Their motive had been to acquire blood money. Their father, Nicholas Newell had been a Lloyd's underwriter and as such was liable following the Lloyd's collapse, for losses in excess of £30,000 a year. The only way that Roderick and Mark could ensure that an inheritance would come their way would be if both their parents were to die. For their insurance policies would cover any losses. Roderick, a former Lieutenant in the Green Jackets, received two life sentences for the murder of his parents. Mark, a city financier, was jailed for six years by the Royal Jersey Court for helping his brother to bury the bodies.

Following the birthday dinner at the Sea Crest Hotel the family had returned to their bungalow, where they had drinks. The police found three glasses on the coffee table in the sitting-room when they searched the house. A heated row followed. Roderick then beat and hacked the couple to death with a rice flail and mattock which he had acquired the day before the killings. His mother was murdered in the master bedroom; his father in the sitting-room. The court heard how the bodies had been wrapped in bags and then driven away from the murder scene in a red Renault van, which had been hired the day before the crime took place. They were buried in a four-foot grave in a remote field at Gréve de Lecq near to where the boys had grown up, on the north-west side of the island.

I find this part of my work very stimulating. If I can help people to get to the truth of what has happened in their lives and relieve some of their anguish it makes my work seem all the more worthwhile. Unfortunately, some people aren't always so open to my methods, but I hope that in the future this will change. There are many cases on which I have worked that I cannot speak about. It could be that the perpetrators of some crimes are yet to be brought to justice, as they have yet to be tracked down, or enough substantive evidence has get to be found, or the case may be currently before the courts. However, I know I have come a long way since my terrifying encounter in the kitchen at Doe Lea. Over the years I have learnt not to fear my gift, but to see the good that it can do. My only wish now is that other people will share this view.

Eleven

LOSING A FRIEND

THROUGH MY work over the years I have come into contact with a great many famous people. To be honest, their 'fame' doesn't mean very much to me. When you do what I do you come to realize that we are all the same, it doesn't matter who you are. We all have the same worries, problems, highs and lows. The press like to call people in the public eye Very Important People. But, as I always say *you* read for a woman who has lost both her little children in a road accident, or talk to someone in their early thirties trying to come to terms with the fact that they have only months to live, then ask yourself who the VIPs really are.

However, and perhaps because I am known to offer the same professional service to all my clients, whoever they are, and treat our encounter as confidential, a number of 'VIPs' started to contact me over the years. Little snippets used to crop up in the papers repeating rumours (often starting, I believe, with friends of friends of the people I might have read for) of my clients, but if the press called me to ask if there was any truth in the story I always laughed it off.

My first contact with Diana, Princess of Wales, happened in 1994. I have never betrayed a client's confidence, and even more than anyone I have always promised to myself and to others that I would never discuss our relationship. Diana was a true friend and a good woman, and one that I would always remain nothing but loyal to.

However, the deep inaccuracy of recent stories published in the press, both national and international, have meant that I am now forced to break my silence for the first time, if only to set the record straight. I feel compelled to tell the truth now that so many lies have been printed, and I want to give to others an insight into the woman I came to know through my work, and grew to love as a friend. I often spoke to Diana every few days, for three years, and we came to know each other very well. I want to show Diana here as I knew her, and offer this as a portrait and a tribute to her. It is all I want to say about her, and all I will ever do.

Diana and I shared a mutual friend, a person for whom I had been reading. During their conversations they had spoken about these readings and the work I did. Diana was evidently curious, although back then I do not think that she fully believed in it all. Our friend arranged that I should give her a telephone reading. We got on very well.

As time passed, she began telephoning me more frequently. Sometimes she would call me for a reading, but more often than not she would simply ring to see how I was. We became friends, but it was to take a whole year before we actually met in person. Understandably, Diana first had to know that she was really able to trust me. Once that had been established, it was never questioned.

Diana actually drove up with her secretary from London to my house in Derbyshire. Before she arrived I remember feeling terribly nervous, although we had sometimes spoken on the phone for hours at a time. I suppose in many ways I had come to treat her just as I would anyone else who rang me for a reading and with whom I had struck up a firm relationship. Even by that time, she was not the woman in the papers, the princess I saw on television, but simply Diana, a warm, friendly, down-to-earth young woman. And yet now that she was coming to my house I couldn't really believe it, it *was* suddenly strange.

As it turned out I had nothing to worry about. As soon as the car pulled up she leapt from it, ran up the pathway, and flung her arms around me. She had been driving the car herself, and thought it hilarious that she had gone

three hours without being spotted. She was also determined not to park in the drive, but out in the street.

'At last, Rita!' she cried as she embraced me. That was
Diana, through and through. Impulsive, affectionate, with
this great gift of being able to put anyone at ease. She was
dressed casually in jeans, a plain shirt, with a cardigan
draped over her shoulders. She was wearing sunglasses as
she came in, but apparently no make-up. She looked
different from the Diana you knew through the media.
She was beautiful of course, yet so natural, so warm and so
seemingly relaxed. It may sound strange but the main
thing that struck me then was how 'normal' she was.

Once inside the house we sat down for coffee. She had
bought me an enormous heart-shaped red velvet box of
chocolates which she unwrapped and offered to me. 'Go
on, have one,' she said. 'I'm going to!' I hadn't known
what to get in for her – she had said all she needed was
bananas and coffee. So I had bought a big bowlful of fruit
with enough bananas to feed ten monkeys and a great big
pineapple. As we sat there chatting away it was as if we
had known each other for years. She was as familiar as one
of my daughters' friends, relaxed and quite at home.

We were in my reading room. She was drinking her
coffee and eating a banana, her foot tapping away excitedly. I must have been staring at her – and I know I was
thinking 'The Princess of Wales is sitting here, in *my*

house!' She suddenly burst out laughing, as if reading my mind, 'Yes Rita, it's really me!'

'I'm so sorry . . .' I said, trying to apologize.

'Oh, don't worry, everyone stares when they first meet me!'

At one point during the conversation Diana knocked her cup, and some coffee spilt on to the carpet. She was aghast.

'I'm so sorry!' she cried. 'You must let me pay for a new carpet.'

'Oh, it's suffered much worse,' I replied.

I admitted to her that I had been nervous about meeting her face to face.

'I'm not sure which one of us is more nervous,' she said. From that moment on I felt very comfortable with her.

Diana was special not only because of who she was in a social context, but because of who she was as a person in her own right. As so many have commented, she had a way with people, an understanding of them that transcended her status, and this was reflected in both her work and her personal life. She knew what it meant to *give*. From a few moments of her time, to placing her hand on someone's shoulder, she understood how people need each other. When she was speaking to you, you knew that she really listened. She would often stare at the floor while you were talking and then suddenly lift her eyes up and ask you a direct question. Then you would know how she had been taking everything in, and how much she cared. She was of course terribly beautiful, especially when she was laughing, but Diana's beauty was not just about her clothes or her figure: it came from within. You could see that in her eyes.

That day I took her round my house. It's a family-sized detached house with a big garden set on the crest of a hill in a small village. I have always thought it to be rather large but I was suddenly conscious that she might think it a bit pokey! 'I bet it's different from Kensington Palace,' I joked. 'Yes, Rita, it is,' she said with almost a sigh, 'but it's your home, it's you, and I love it.' She wanted to see the whole of it, from my bedroom to the kitchen, to a stroll around my garden. There was nothing patronizing or grand about her, she didn't make me feel embarrassed about anything, however different it was to what she knew. She also wanted to know all about my family and my life and took great interest in everything she saw around her. My gypsy ornaments, trinkets and china amused her. To be honest, I don't think she had come across anything like them before. 'Your bits and bobs,' she used to call them.

In my reading room, she looked intently at the hundreds of photographs of the spirit children that line the walls. They are photographs of children who have passed into the spirit world, given to me by their families. She must have spent over half an hour poring over them, taking in every little face. 'Aren't they sweet,' she said as she turned to look at me. I realized she was crying. 'How I admire you,' she said.

Diana had already been to a couple of psychics and astrologers before she started seeing me. When the press and her critics found out about these they would always be terribly negative about it all, seeing it as a bad thing. But the point is that Diana was a very spiritual person. She consulted people like me because she was trying to make sense of things not only in terms of her difficult personal life but because of her remarkable work too. For a woman of only thirty-six years Diana had seen more suffering and grief, death and trauma than many of us can begin to imagine. After every such encounter she would take this home with her, she couldn't just walk away from it. She was a very sensitive person, who felt things deeply.

Often Diana would call me up just to tell me what she had been through that day, about the people she had seen, what their lives must be like. And so nothing made Diana happier than knowing there *was* more than this life, that there was an afterlife. As I've said before, when she originally came to me I am not sure that she fully believed in what I did, but she was open and curious. She did not accept things just like that; she would always ask questions and liked to talk things through.

Like me, Diana was a Cancer. As people I've read for know, I do think star signs are a useful and generally accurate way of looking at personality types. Cancers are typically home-lovers who have a hard shell but a soft centre, people who are very much in control of themselves, and people who feel very much for other people – which can sometimes cause them problems. Perhaps this is why we got on: maybe we understood each other at this level. We had both seen a lot of heartache through our work, and somehow had to learn how to deal with it. She shared my belief: 'We Cancers must stick together, Rita!', she always used to say.

In another life Diana would have made the most wonderful nurse. I once said this to her. 'I would have loved that, Rita,' she said. And before she passed over she told me that she wanted to set up hospices round the world. 'Do you think that's a good idea?' she asked me. 'Yes,' I told her, 'It's a *wonderful* idea.' It certainly wasn't a passing remark, it was something that she had thought long and hard about. But Diana already had a role, an important one – not as a princess, but as a mother. She put this first – before everything. She was very maternal, and she loved her children more than words can express.

She would talk about 'My boys' with great pride – for hours if she could. They were her true life.

The caring side of Diana was not something that she cultivated simply because of her public role. It was instinctive, and went beyond the realms of her charity work. In private, with her friends, she was just the same. I suffer from osteoporosis. Over the years it has become a chronic condition, one that often leaves me quite unable to move or fulfil the most basic daily task. Diana obviously understood this. 'I can't bear to think of you in pain,' she would say. If I was ever going through a bad patch she would call me every day to find out how I was getting on and offer her support. If it was very bad, sometimes I didn't tell her, so as not to worry her.

For some reason, we were chatting on the phone one day about having a bath, of all things. Because of my osteoporosis I had not been able to have a bath for years, since getting in and out of the wretched thing had become impossible.

'What on earth do you do without a soak?' she asked.

'I have showers instead,' I replied.

'But that's not the same.'

A week later, without my knowledge, she had arranged for a specially-fitted disabled person's bath to be installed in my home. I was moved to tears. With it came a box filled with bubble bath and some yellow rubber ducks. She called me the day it was put in, very excited. 'Take your portable phone into the bathroom with you, I want to talk to you while you have your first bath!' I did as I was told. We were both laughing our heads off. 'Ready for the launch?' she cried, just as I was about to get in. 'I hope you're not referring to my size there!' I teased her back. She couldn't stop laughing. The next time she came to my house the first thing she did was rush straight to the bathroom to see it.

The smallest gestures could mean so much. She would, for instance, always call to say that she had arrived safely after setting off on a trip, and she would always send cards and letters. She once sent me a lovely scented candle as a present. I was very touched and treasured it for it was very beautiful, placing it in the middle of my dining table as a centrepiece. I had never had one before, and I decided not to take the wrapping off in case it got dirty. But when Diana next came and saw it there, all wrapped up, she fell about laughing. 'Oh, you are a silly goose, Rita! Honestly, you're supposed to *use* it!' she said, tearing off the cellophane.

Diana loved to joke around with people, and loved a tease. She used to find all my Derbyshire expressions extremely funny, especially when I would say things like 'Oh, I've been driven up the wall and down the other side' by someone or something. 'Oh stop it, Rita! You're making me laugh too much,' she'd say. She called me 'the Lady from the North', and we always joked about the differences between the north and the south of England. One afternoon, on her last visit in August 1997, she picked up my pet tortoise. 'I didn't know you were into this kind of thing,' she said. 'That's my baby toytoys,' I replied, the way I always pronounce that word. She was soon laughing so much she could barely speak. 'That's a *tortoise* Rita, not a "toytoys".'

Diana called me her friend. 'Rita, I love you, you do know that don't you?' she would say. Even though we were worlds apart, she a princess and I a psychic with a gypsy heritage, there seemed to be an extraordinary bond between us. She wasn't ashamed of me, of who I am or what I do. When the press rumours started about our friendship with all her critics joining ranks, and as I was feeling uncomfortable about how this might make her feel, she used to say, 'I don't care what they say, Rita. You're my friend. I'm not embarrassed.' I remember a few times when she even called me from her mobile phone while she was out jogging! Once, she was giggling away because she had just bought an ice cream from a van in the park where she was running. Realizing who she was, the ice cream man hadn't wanted to charge her, but she had insisted on paying. Another time, I was looking out of the window while she was talking and could see the daylight was going. I went on at her like an anxious mother – 'You make sure you're home before it gets dark!'

Sometimes a month would go by without Diana calling, at other times she would call three or four times a week. But these calls were not always readings. Often she would just ring for a chat, to find out how I was, to talk about her plans or just what was going on in her life. She liked to hear about the people I read for, if I was free to talk about them, to hear the stories of those who said I could share them. Many of those are included here in this book. She would always ask after the people she had heard about, and want to know how they were coping. She respected what I did, the comfort which I could bring people through my work. 'I admire your strength and calmness' she once wrote to me. 'And the TLC [tender loving care] which you give so many people.'

But Diana certainly did not rely on me or my readings, in any way. She was a very strong person, wilful and capable of making her own mind up about life. The readings I gave her interested her, and I hope gave her an inner strength, but she did not come to me to know which path she should take. She would have hated anyone to think that her life was dictated by what I or anyone else would say to her. Diana always made her own decisions. If something was bothering her she would often ring me and we would talk it through, and I would try my best to be of help to her. She did ask my advice about the famous *Panorama* interview and I supported her choice. Diana consulted me more as a friend, somebody who really understood her, than as a medium.

Despite all she had been through, Diana was never bitter. During the last few years of her life she had learnt to accept many things. You could always tell if she was upset about something or someone, or if she was worried or hurt, because she would just go quiet when the subject came up. But in those last months before she passed away there were no such moments, and I felt I had watched her become a much more spiritual person over the time I had known her. She was radiantly happy, loving life, and full of it. Her conversations were all joy and laughter, and full of excitement about everything that was going on.

The last time I saw Diana was on 12 August 1997. She came, with her friend Dodi Fayed, from London in a Harrods helicopter. I was not expecting *her* that day at all. We had arranged a week before that I would read for Dodi, and that he would come and see me on his own. Diana had said that she did not think that she would be able to come herself as she had many appointments to keep.

We knew that Dodi would be coming by helicopter. It

is quite a long journey to make, and he had said that he did not have much time either, but he did want to meet me, as a friend of Diana's. I suggested that he might land at the local airstrip and that we would come and fetch him in the car, but he told us not to worry about that because the helicopter would be able to land in the paddock Diana had told him was behind my house. He said that the pilot would call us on the telephone just before they were due to land, to let us know to look out for them.

But when the call came through it was not the pilot on the line but Diana. 'Surprise, Surprise!' she cried, imitating Cilla Black. 'Oh Rita, I'm sorry to intrude, but you don't think for one minute I could resist the chance of coming to see you, do you? I had to come along with Dodi so I could see you again!' It took them quite a while to land as they couldn't find the field. In the end Mo had to mark out an 'H' shape in the field with emulsion paint, and lit a pile of leaves and grass clippings to create a smoke signal. Once they had safely landed we went into the garden to meet them. It was a very hot day so we had tea on the patio, and sat there chatting for a while. Then Diana said, 'Right Dodi, you go off with Rita now and I'll wait out here.'

I led Dodi into the reading room. He was an attractive, gentle man, with beautiful manners. 'I am glad to meet you at last, Mrs Rogers,' he had said when we were introduced. This wasn't actually Dodi's first reading with me. I had spoken to him on several occasions already while he was staying on his yacht, the *Jonikal*, earlier in the summer.

As Dodi knew, I had told Diana in a reading shortly after I first knew her that she would meet a man with whom she would fall in love, and that they would be together on a boat. When she had called me during the summer and asked, 'Guess where I am, Rita?' I had had no idea, since she was always off all over the place, going to locations I had never even heard of. 'I'm in the Mediterranean. With a man on a boat!' she said excitedly. 'Rita you forecasted this, you said that this would happen.' As Diana had told Dodi that I had predicted that they would meet he was very keen to speak to me, and he also wanted a reading. And so Diana had asked me if I would give him an initial telephone reading from the boat.

Dodi was extremely grateful when I agreed to this, and the reading went well – he told me afterwards that he was impressed. But even during that first reading I sensed that there was something not quite right about his life. I had a feeling of danger, and that it had something to do with a car. Indeed, the feeling was so strong that I was prompted to ask him whether he had been in a serious car accident before. He said that he hadn't, but that he would be sure to be careful in future. I also felt that there was a problem with his security. He said that he would see to it. He seemed to take what I said seriously.

Diana called me later to say Dodi had been very impressed by the reading, and had started telling everyone about it. Dodi said that he would like to come and see me in person when he was back in England, which is why we made this appointment. Some people say that when mediums see danger or have bad news about a person they keep it to themselves. Now, there are no accepted rules governing what a medium can or cannot say to the person they are reading for; in my experience if you are told something by a spirit it is your duty to pass it on, but up to you to convey the message in the right way for that person. After all, if the spirits tell me something in a reading it is because they *want* you to know; the message is not for me, I am only the medium. In situations like this one was, where an accident is involved, the spirit may be sending you a message about it as a warning, because it is something that may be avoidable. Again, all I can do is pass on that warning. I cannot stop something from happening once that person has walked out of my reading room. It is up to the person, where possible, to take heed of what has been said. Of course, this is often very difficult, especially as no specific time frames are usually given.

When Dodi came to see me that August afternoon, I

was still filled with this terrible sense of danger and foreboding. If anything, it was now much stronger than it had been when I read for him over the telephone.

The image of the car would not go away. The car I was seeing was black. A voice was telling me the word 'Mercedes'. The car was not Dodi's, though – I felt sure of that. It belonged to someone else. I could also see a tunnel and water and I felt that there was a connection with France. I repeated this all to Dodi. He seemed to be taking it all in, listening carefully but calmly, his head resting back on his hands, his arms stretched out. I asked him to be very careful.

'I will,' he said. 'I will.' And then he said, 'She is very precious to me.'

Some people have argued that if I was any good as a medium what happened at the end of that August would never have happened. But as I said earlier, all I can do is warn people. I can pass on spirit messages, but I cannot control events. After the accident so many people asked me whether I had predicted it or not. I decided there and then not to answer the question. Posthumous predictions are of little use to anyone, and I still believe this to be true. I am saying what I am saying now because I feel forced to speak out. So many lies have been printed and broadcast about what I did and didn't say. I have even seen stories about a reading I am purported to have given

Diana that August day, which despite everything does make me laugh since I never did read for her that day, nor indeed had done so for some time. How anyone could possibly have known what was or was not said within the confines of my reading room not only bewilders me but angers me; it has caused distress not just to myself but to the families of both Diana and Dodi. Everything that was said about the accident is printed here. I only feel able to share as much as I am saying of what I told Dodi: for he himself discussed the reading widely in France over the next weeks.

Dodi Fayed was very much in love with Diana. Whatever people said had happened in his past had become irrelevant. I think that all his life Dodi had been waiting for a *special* person, and that summer he had truly found her. When he said 'She is very precious to me,' I felt he had really meant it. I had even told Dodi that I felt he would never have another girlfriend. 'I know,' he said. 'She is the one.' He went on to explain how in love with her he was, and not only did he adore her, but he admired her and he respected her. He wanted to look after her, to protect her.

*

By the time the reading had ended Diana was getting very fidgety out on the patio. 'I really think we should go,' she said. She was always very aware of being caught out, and seemed instinctively to know when her privacy was going to be intruded upon. We made our way to the helicopter in the paddock and were saying our goodbyes when Diana spotted a group of children looking on. She ran back to my arms. 'They've seen me and they've got a camera,' she said. The next day, of course, the pictures were printed in newspapers all around the world. But I was surprised to read that Diana had shouted at the children to go away – it had been me! Even so, I was not to know then what the repercussions of those photographs were to be.

The last I saw of her was her face in the helicopter window, her hand waving. When I went back into the house I went to my bedroom. Lying there on my pillow was a gift from Diana, together with a handwritten note. It read 'You're simply the best. With all my love and kisses and a big hug, Diana.'

Although the children's photograph of us standing by the helicopter in the paddock was sold and published in the papers the following day Diana did not seem that upset about it for her own sake. By now she was used to it. In the months before she had realized that the press were not going to leave her and Dodi alone. But what she was upset about was the effect that it was having on me. She knew that I hated this sort of exposure, as I did not want to be seen as deliberately associating myself with her. 'Why does my presence always seem to make so much trouble for other people?' she said to me later that week. 'Because everyone loves you, they all want to get whatever glimpse they can of you,' I replied.

But in a few short hours my life and Mo's became a misery. I felt hounded, a prisoner in my own home, with journalists everywhere, from all over the world, even camping outside my garden wall front and back waiting for me to speak. I was adamant that I wouldn't. Nevertheless, the strain of it all was becoming too much for me. I even broke a vertebrae falling to my knees to avoid having my picture taken through my reading room window. Finding it very difficult to cope, I had to cancel my readings. My clients were unable to come to the door or reach me by telephone anyway, due to the incessant seige and phone calls from more journalists. My family was very upset by it all. Our local policeman had to try and usher the reporters away every night, and one reporter even took off with my pet tortoise. 'If this is what it's like now for me, imagine what her life is like,' I kept thinking. But I did not want to speak to the press about her, and she knew that. She called every day to make sure I was OK.

'Oh Rita, I'm sorry,' she said to me. 'If only I could put this right . . .'

She called me from Paris on the afternoon of 30 August. It was 4.30 p.m. in England. She was terribly happy, and told me how much she had loved her holiday with Dodi. She told me that she had discovered that Dodi had gone out to collect a ring for her. She was in love, there was no denying that. But the real reason for all the joy and excitement in her voice was because she was about to be reunited with her boys. She told me that she was having dinner at the Ritz that night. She was thrilled about it. I was pleased she was happy, but I couldn't share her enthusiasm. You see, I had not wanted her to go to Paris in the first place.

'Do be careful,' I said.

'Why did you say that?' she asked.

'It's just a feeling, you know.'

'Oh Rita, of course I'll be careful, I promise, I promise. I'll ring you when I get back home.' With that, she hung up.

*

I was telephoned by a close friend of hers at 1 a.m. the following morning with the news that she had been involved in a terrible accident. I cannot begin to describe how I felt. I don't suppose anyone can. I just felt so sad, so awfully sad. I tried to look back and see whether there was anything that I could have done which would have changed the course of events. I wanted someone to tell me that there had been a mistake, that it hadn't happened. Even now I sometimes can't really believe it. I keep expecting it to be her when the telephone rings – 'Hello Rita, it's only me.' After I heard the news I went into my bathroom and just stood there for a while. I took a deep breath, and as I did so I felt that I could smell her perfume. It was like a breath of air. And then it was gone.

I decided not to go to London for her funeral, although some of her friends asked me to attend. You see, I didn't want to upset anyone by being there. In any case, as I always say, funerals and graves are only for the living, not really for those who have passed away. Instead, I went away for a couple of days, to gather my thoughts about her. It was while I was away that I came to realize what all I had learnt over the years meant in this situation. At last she was safe. Her true spirit was free.

Diana passed over when she was at the happiest point in her life. I had never seen her so radiant or so full of love or joy. She could not help smiling or laughing, for that is how she felt. Her passing is an almost unbearable loss for us all, especially for her sons and her family. But her spirit will always live on.

All Pan Books are available at your local bookshop or newsagent, or can be ordered direct from the publisher. Indicate the number of copies required and fill in the form below.

Send to: Macmillan General Books C.S.
Book Service By Post
PO Box 29, Douglas I-O-M
IM99 1BQ

or phone: 01624 675137, quoting title, author and credit card number.

or fax: 01624 670923, quoting title, author, and credit card number.

or Internet: http://www.bookpost.co.uk

Please enclose a remittance* to the value of the cover price plus 75 pence per book for post and packing. Overseas customers please allow £1.00 per copy for post and packing.

*Payment may be made in sterling by UK personal cheque, Eurocheque, postal order, sterling draft or international money order, made payable to Book Service By Post.

Alternatively by Access/Visa/MasterCard

Card No.
⬜⬜⬜⬜⬜⬜⬜⬜⬜⬜⬜⬜⬜⬜⬜⬜

Expiry Date
⬜⬜⬜⬜⬜⬜⬜⬜⬜⬜⬜⬜⬜⬜⬜⬜

Signature _____

Applicable only in the UK and BFPO addresses.

While every effort is made to keep prices low, it is sometimes necessary to increase prices at short notice. Pan Books reserve the right to show on covers and charge new retail prices which may differ from those advertised in the text or elsewhere.

NAME AND ADDRESS IN BLOCK CAPITAL LETTERS PLEASE

Name _____

Address _____

_____

_____

_____

8/95

Please allow 28 days for delivery.
Please tick box if you do not wish to receive any additional information. ⬜